CHAMPIONS OF FAITH

Great Stories VOLUME 2 of the Bible

CONQUERING HEROES

Merlin L. Neff

Pacific Press® Publishing Association
Nampa, Idaho
Oshawa, Ontario, Canada
www.pacificpress.com

Cover design by Gerald Lee Monks
Cover illustration by Clyde Provonsha
Inside design by Steve Lanto

All Scriptures quoted are from The New King James Version,
copyright © 1979, 1980, 1982, Thomas Nelson, Inc., Publishers.

Library of Congress Cataloging-in-Publication Data

Neff, Merlin L.
Conquering heroes / Merlin L. Neff.
p. cm.
ISBN-10: 0-8163-2265-1
ISBN-13: 978-0-8163-2265-7 (hard cover)
1. Bible stories, English.—O.T. 2. Bible
O.T.—Biography—Juvenile
literature. I. Title.
BS551.3.N445 2008
221.9'505—dc22
                              2008002461

Additional copies of this book are available by calling toll-free
1-800-765-6955 or by visiting http://www.adventistbookcenter.com.

08 09 10 11 12 • 5 4 3 2 1

"Train up a child in the way he should go, and when he is old he will not depart from it."

—Proverbs 22:6

Interior Illustrations:

Robert Ayres: pages 8, 152.
Norman Brice: pages 32, 33, 132.
Lars Justinen: page 61.
John Lear: page 64.
Joe Maniscalco: pages 28, 52, 53, 65, 80, 92, 96, 120, 124, 133, 141, 144, 148, 160.
Clyde Provonsha: pages 1, 37, 40, 44, 45, 56, 72.
John Steel: pages 9, 12, 16, 17, 20, 24, 25, 48, 77, 85, 97, 102, 106, 117, 135, 156, 157.
Helen Torrey: page 21.

CONTENTS

FOR PARENTS

Pass Your Values On to Your Children
Through Bible Stories

A s a parent, you likely want your nine- or ten- or eleven-year-old daughter or son to enter the teen years knowing the most important stories of the Bible. As you look for ways to pass on to your child the love of God and the principles that represent His character, consider how well a good story captures the attention of human beings of all ages. The Bible stories in these five volumes will place God's principles in your child's mind in such a way that they won't forget them as they grow older.

Read these books with your child—or have the child read the story to you—morning or evening or Sabbath afternoon, every week. This is a good way to build your child's character and faith in God without your having to explain a bunch of abstract ideas. Their awareness of how God works with His people will grow without their realizing it.

Every generation through history that forgot about the Scriptures, and therefore the knowledge and implementation of God's principles, has suffered greatly from its own evil and self-destructive actions. A similar destiny awaits the children of this generation if we fail to bring the stories of the Bible to bear on their lives. The stakes are too high, the dangers too close, for us to neglect the story of salvation as we raise our children.

The timeless truths of the Bible come through clearly in the stories of this five-volume set. Each story has been screened for some elements more suited to adult readers. The stories chosen are the ones that follow the thread of salvation down through the centuries. In places where people of the Bible speak to each other, the words are quoted from the New King James Version, which is fairly easy to understand and widely accepted.

Pray for your child that he or she will respond positively when the Holy Spirit speaks to his or her heart. These Bible stories may bring your child to a turning point of knowing God in their own experience and accepting His love and His principles. There is supernatural power in the Word of God that may change your son or daughter forever.

The Publisher

THE SON OF A PRINCESS

Exodus 1–2:10

Slave! The word stung Amram as he said it over and over. He remembered how the soldier had struck him with a whip and called him a "slave of Pharaoh." His people, the descendants of Jacob, had been in Egypt about 150 years, tending their cows and sheep in the land of Goshen. In earlier years, they had been well liked by the rulers of the country, but now they were despised. New kings had come to the throne who did not remember Joseph, the wise governor who had once saved Egypt from famine.

Amram was a descendant of Levi, the third son of Jacob. He knew the history of his people—how Joseph had been sold as a slave by his brothers; how father Jacob, a brave adventurer, had made the long journey to Egypt with his family to save them from the famine in Canaan; how God had told Jacob that his children would someday return to their Promised Land.

But many years had passed and the Israelites, as Jacob's people were called, were still in Egypt. They could no longer live peacefully as shepherds, because they were being treated as slaves who must obey the orders of a hard-hearted pharaoh.

Jacob's family had grown until his descendants filled the land of Goshen. Pharaoh did not like to have these strong, clever foreigners so near him. If they were not crushed, he thought they might someday take control of all Egypt. He ordered his soldiers to raid the homes of the Israelites and force the men to work for no pay, building temples and cities or laboring in the fields where wheat, barley, and flax were grown.

GOD SAYS:

"The more they afflicted them, the more they multiplied and grew. And they were in dread of the children of Israel." -Exodus 1:12

When the soldiers came for Amram, he left his house with a heavy heart. He and his wife, Jochebed, had two children, a daughter, Miriam, and a little son, Aaron. They were expecting another baby soon. Amram was afraid because of a new law Pharaoh had made, that every son born to the people of Jacob should be thrown into the river where hungry crocodiles swam.

Amram went with a gang of slaves to the brick fields, where they were forced to make bricks from mud. As the hot days went by, sweat dripped from his body as he kneaded the mud with his hands, shaped the bricks, and laid them in the sun to dry. If only he could rest for a few minutes in the shade. But no, he must keep moving or the guard's whip would make another red welt on his bare back. Some of the men became sick, and when a beating could not force them to work any more, they were left to die. A loud cry went up from the Israelites. It was a prayer asking God to remember His people and deliver them from the tortures of their Egyptian masters.

Many weeks dragged by before Amram was allowed to return home. He hurried along the road, his mind troubled and afraid. He longed to see his wife and children, but he dreaded to think of the news that might be waiting for him if the new baby were a boy!

Night had come by the time Amram reached his home. As he entered the door, Jochebed ran to meet him. Quickly she whispered her secret in his ear. Yes, they had a new baby—a handsome son! She led her husband to a hiding place and showed him the chubby boy. But the worried man scarcely glanced at the baby. He feared that Pharaoh's soldiers would take his boy, and he felt powerless to stop them. But Amram and Jochebed believed in God's power to help them. They prayed that the Lord would protect their baby and make him a strong leader.

After only a short time, Amram had to go back to his forced labor, and the mother was left with Miriam and Aaron and the baby. When the infant was three months old, he cried so loud that Jochebed knew she could no longer hide him in the house. She called her daughter, Miriam, and together they came up with a plan. They took a basket made of reeds that grew in the river,

QUICK FACT:
Angels helped Pharaoh's daughter find Moses' basket.

covered the outside with a layer of sticky black tar so it would be watertight, and set it in the sun to dry. As

Jochebed went about her work in the house, she could not forget the basket in the yard. When she looked at it, she wondered if it would be possible to save her little son.

Early the next morning Miriam and her mother carried the basket to an isolated place on the Nile River and put it in the water. Jochebed watched carefully to see if water would seep into the basket, but it remained dry inside. Miriam ran back to the house and soon returned carrying her baby brother in a blanket. Tenderly the mother tucked him into the basket and covered him up. She wondered if she would ever see her son again. After praying for God to protect her child, she pushed the basket out among the tall papyrus grass and reeds in the water, where it rocked gently on the waves. Jochebed knew that if the basket floated out into the strong current, it might overturn.

Miriam sat down near the bank of the river to watch the precious basket. The mother did not dare remain there, because her presence might attract the soldiers.

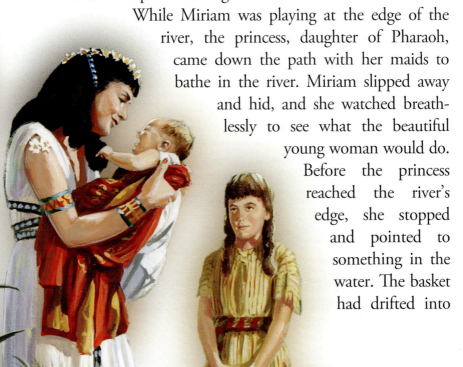

While Miriam was playing at the edge of the river, the princess, daughter of Pharaoh, came down the path with her maids to bathe in the river. Miriam slipped away and hid, and she watched breathlessly to see what the beautiful young woman would do.

Before the princess reached the river's edge, she stopped and pointed to something in the water. The basket had drifted into plain sight. Perhaps Pharaoh's daughter thought it was an idol that someone had set afloat in the river as a gift to the god of the Nile. Calling one of her maids, she commanded that the basket be brought to her. When she opened it, there was a crying baby! The princess took the child in her arms and rocked him gently. She realized that a desperate mother was attempting to save her baby's life in this strange way.

"This is one of the Hebrews' children," she said. The Egyptians called the Israelites *Hebrews,* which means "foreigners."

Now Miriam, who had been watching the princess, came close to her and asked, "Shall I go and call a nurse for you from the Hebrew women, that she may nurse the child for you?"

"Go," said Pharaoh's daughter to her.

So Miriam ran and told her mother what had happened, and Jochebed hurried to the river and bowed before the king's daughter. The princess placed the baby in the woman's arms, saying, "Take this child away and nurse him for me, and I will give you your wages."

Jochebed and Amram were very thankful to God for His wonderful answer to their prayers. Now they were able to love and care for their own son under the protection of the royal family. Time with the boy would be precious, because he would soon be taken from them by the princess. Jochebed spent many hours teaching her son about the true God who created the earth. She told him of the pioneers, Abraham, Isaac, and Jacob, who had loved and obeyed the Lord. Over and over the boy listened to the promise of how the Israelites would be delivered.

When the boy was about twelve years old, Jochebed took him to the palace, and the princess adopted him. She gave him an Egyptian name, Moses, "because I drew him out of the water," she said.

A wonderful new world opened up before Moses. Like Joseph long before, this young man was suddenly honored in the court of the pharaohs. Instead of living in a small house, he now lived in a magnificent palace. Around him were imposing statues, rich paintings, and furniture of ivory and gold. Moses, clothed in fine linen garments embroidered in many colors, rode in a royal chariot. He learned to read and write under the guidance of the wisest teachers of Egypt, and as he grew older he studied history, science, art, and music. He became a general, carefully trained to lead the Egyptian army. Moses the prince, educated in the Egyptian culture, might someday be the king of the mighty nation on the Nile River.

THOUGHT QUESTION:

Why did Moses refuse to worship the Egyptian gods?

However, all the riches and splendor of the cities and temples of Egypt did not dazzle this young man. He refused to worship the many gods honored by the Egyptians. He never forgot his home and what his parents had taught him about the true God. The terrible slavery of his people troubled him greatly. He prayed that they might soon have their freedom, so that they could return to the land of Canaan that God have given Abraham. But what could he, a prince in the court of Pharaoh, do to help the Israelites gain their freedom? He dreamed of being a mighty conqueror. Someday God would make that dream come true, but in a way that Moses could not have imagined.

ESCAPE FROM DEATH

Exodus 2:11–4:31

W hen Prince Moses was about forty years old, he went
out of the court of Pharaoh one day, determined to
see how his fellow Israelites were being treated. He decided
to drive his chariot down the road toward the land of Goshen to visit his family and see his boyhood friends. On the
way he noticed a group of Hebrew slaves building a city for
the king. Huge blocks of stone were being dragged into
place by thousands of laborers. The sun beat down on the
men, and many were crying for mercy. Moses went on his
way feeling sad and upset. He had not gone much farther
when he came upon an Egyptian guard beating a Hebrew
slave unmercifully. He became very angry when he remembered the many times his own father had been whipped
while he labored for Pharaoh. *Perhaps this is the time for me
to rescue my people,* he said to himself.

Jumping from his chariot, Moses ran and grabbed the
guard. The whimpering slave scrambled away in terror
when he saw the young prince. The man with the whip
attempted to fight, but Moses struck him a fierce blow

and knocked him to the ground. As the prince gazed at the fallen guard, he realized what he had done. The man was dead! Moses looked in every direction to see if anyone had seen him. But no one was nearby, and the beaten slave had disappeared. Quickly he dug a hole in the sand, buried the dead man, and drove off in his chariot.

The next day, while he was riding through the same part of the country, Moses passed two Israelites quarreling. He stopped and came back to speak to the one who was hitting his fellow slave. "Why are you striking your companion?" Moses asked.

The man who had hit the other Israelite looked at Moses and recognized him as the prince. Then he replied, "Who

made you a prince and a judge over us? Do you intend to kill me as you killed the Egyptian?"

When Moses heard these words, he was shocked. He drove quickly away, miserable and afraid. The news of the Egyptian guard's death must have spread everywhere. When he returned to the palace, he discovered that the story had reached the ears of Pharaoh and that the angry king was determined to take his life. Moses now had to make a fateful choice. He could renounce his people and take his permanent place with the Egyptians. That way he could, perhaps, save himself from Pharaoh's wrath. Or he could stand with his people, give up his right to the throne, and run away from Egypt.

Moses made his decision quickly. Because he had

faith in God's plan, he "refused to be called the son of Pharaoh's daughter, choosing rather to suffer affliction with the people of God than to enjoy the passing pleasures of sin" (Hebrews 11:24, 25).

And he had to act immediately. That night he fled from the palace, crossed the Nile River, and headed south through the desert. The riches, the pleasures, and the glory of Egypt would never be his again.

THOUGHT QUESTION:

Why did Moses kill the Egyptian guard?

Tired and hungry after days of travel, Moses stopped one afternoon at a well in the land of Midian. This was a country of great open spaces, with no cities and no blood-thirsty kings. Here he found peace and quiet, and God seemed very near. As Moses sat in the shade of a palm tree, he saw seven young women coming toward the well with a flock of sheep. They drew water from the well and filled the troughs so that the animals could drink. But some selfish shepherds, who wanted to water their flocks first, drove the sheep away. When Moses saw that the young women were not able to protect their flock, he came to their rescue and watered the sheep for them.

The seven young women were sisters. When they returned home, their father, Jethro, asked, "How is it that you have come [back] so soon today?" One of the sisters replied, "An Egyptian delivered us from the hand of the shepherds, and he also drew enough water for us and watered the flock."

"And where is he?" asked Jethro, who was a priest of Midian. He was always kind to strangers. "Why is it that you have left the man? Call him, that he may eat bread."

Moses happily accepted the hospitality of this good man and thanked God for a place of refuge. The family welcomed him, and Jethro offered Moses a home with them. In this way Prince Moses became a sheepherder, living with a tribe of shepherds in that desert country.

Moses fell in love with Zipporah, one of Jethro's seven daughters, and after a time the couple were married. For many years Moses was content to live in the desert, far from the threat of enemies. The man who had once been a privileged member of the Egyptian royal family now camped in a tent, moving from place to place to find pasture for the sheep. Moses grew to love the quietness and beauty of the desert. Around him bare mountains lifted their scarred peaks, and jagged cliffs reflected the heat of the sun. The land was calm and still; scarcely a leaf moved. Away from the noise and temptations of the cities, Moses learned to love God and to understand the wonders of nature. Having been trained as a soldier, he now learned how to be humble and patient while tending the sheep.

One day, when Moses had taken the flocks to pastureland near Mount Horeb, he saw a strange sight. A bush was blazing with fire, yet its trunk, branches, and leaves were not burned up. As the shepherd stood watching the flames and wondering about this mystery, God spoke to him, calling, "Moses, Moses!"

"Here I am!" he said.

"Do not draw near this place," said the Lord. "Take your sandals off your feet,

Quick Fact: The forty years Moses spent as a shepherd in the desert helped prepare him to lead the Israelite people.

for the place where you stand is holy ground." It was the custom of that country for people to take off their shoes when they were in a sacred place as a way to show reverence.

Moses realized he was in the presence of God, so he took off his shoes and covered his face. Listening intently, he heard the voice of the Lord say, "I have surely seen the oppression of My people who are in Egypt, and have heard their cry because of their taskmasters, for I know their sorrows. So I have come down to deliver them out of the hand of the Egyptians. . . . Come now, therefore, and I will send you to Pharaoh that you may bring My people, the children of Israel, out of Egypt."

When Moses heard that God was calling him to lead his people, he was afraid. He had failed so dismally the first time he attempted to rescue them. He thought about the enemies in the court of Egypt who might be waiting for him if he came back, even though the pharaoh who had threatened to kill him was dead. Moses was sure it would be very difficult to free the people of Israel.

"Who am I that I should go to Pharaoh, and that I should bring the children of Israel out of Egypt?" Moses asked.

"I will certainly be with you," God said. "And this shall be a sign to you that I have sent you: When you have brought the people out of Egypt, you shall serve God on this mountain."

Moses was filled with awe. Would his people someday live in this desert land, free from slavery? But as he thought of the enormous task before him, Moses began to make excuses. He said, "Suppose they will not believe me or listen to my voice; suppose they say, 'The Lord has not appeared to you.' "

The Lord said to him, "What is that in your hand?"

"A [shepherd's] rod," he said.

"Cast it on the ground."

Moses threw it on the ground, and it became a snake. He ran from it, but the Lord called him back, saying, "Reach out your hand and take it by the tail."

The shepherd grabbed the snake by the tail, and it turned into a shepherd's staff. This was one of several signs God gave

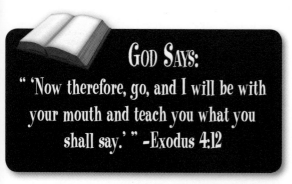

GOD SAYS:

" 'Now therefore, go, and I will be with your mouth and teach you what you shall say.' " -Exodus 4:12

Moses to help him prove to the Israelites that his message was from heaven.

Then Moses thought of another excuse—he was not a good speaker. But the Lord said to him, "I will be with your mouth and teach you what you shall say." Then God promised that Aaron, the elder brother of Moses, would stand by his side as speaker and counselor.

Returning to the tents of Jethro, Moses asked his father-in-law if he could take his wife and two sons to the land of the Nile River.

"Go in peace," said Jethro to his son-in-law.

When Moses and his family were near Egypt, Aaron came out to welcome them. The brothers talked and planned what they would say to Pharaoh. Then Moses and Aaron called the leaders of the Israelite people together and told them that the Lord was going to deliver them from their affliction. Moses performed wonderful acts as God had commanded him to do. When the leaders saw the strange signs, they believed Moses and bowed their heads to God in worship.

Next Moses would have to go to the court of Pharaoh and plead for the Israelites to be freed. Would the king listen to him? He knew that he might be thrown in prison for having killed the Egyptian guard many years before, but he resolved to be true to his task. With Aaron to stand beside him, the prince obeyed God and entered the royal palace to stand before the king.

PLAGUES FALL ON EGYPT

Exodus 5–10

Pharaoh watched as his guards escorted the two Hebrews down the stately halls of the palace toward him. When they bowed before his throne, the king gave them a scornful glance. *They are slaves,* he thought. *Why aren't they working in the brickfields?*

When Moses and Aaron arose from bowing, Moses addressed the monarch in these simple words: "Thus says the Lord God of Israel: 'Let My people go, that they may hold a feast to Me in the wilderness.' "

A shadow of anger crossed Pharaoh's face. He snarled at them, "Who is the Lord, that I should obey His voice to let Israel go? I do not know the Lord, nor will I let Israel go."

Again Moses and Aaron asked that the Israelites be allowed to go into the desert, to offer sacrifices and to worship God for three days. Once more Pharaoh refused. As an excuse for denying their petition, he said, "Moses and Aaron, why do you take the people from their work? Get back to your labor. . . . Look, the people of the land are many now, and you make them rest from their labor!"

The king was afraid that if the Israelites were allowed to go out into the desert, they would never return. They had been tortured and beaten as slaves for so many years that he was certain they would go on to Canaan if they once tasted freedom. When Moses and Aaron left the palace, Pharaoh wasted no time in commanding his guards to increase the work of the slaves. The straw that was essential in making good bricks would no longer be supplied. The Israelites would have to go out into the fields and find stubble. Yet, in spite of this extra work, they would be required to make the same number of bricks each day as before. "Let more work be laid on the men, that they may labor in it, and let them not regard false words," Pharaoh said.

Soon the Israelite leaders went to the king and complained, saying, "Why are you dealing thus with your servants? There is no straw given to your servants, and they say to us, 'Make brick!' And indeed your servants are beaten, but the fault is in your own people."

Pharaoh was very angry at this complaint. "You are idle! You are idle!" he declared. "Therefore you say, 'Let us go and sacrifice to the Lord.' . . . Go

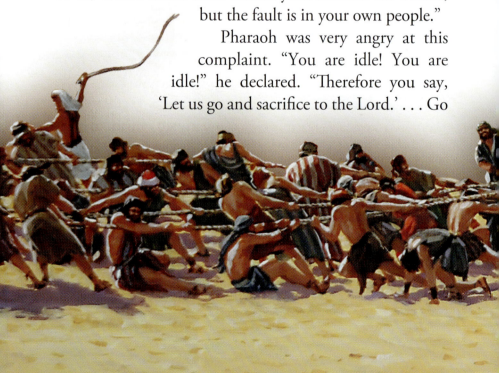

now and work; for no straw shall be given you, yet you shall deliver the [same] quota of bricks."

After the Israelite leaders left the palace, they met Moses and Aaron. They had decided that these two men were the cause of their trouble. To the brothers they said, "Let the Lord look on you and judge, because you have made us abhorrent in the sight of Pharaoh and in the sight of his servants, to put a sword in their hand to kill us!"

Everything seemed to have turned against Moses. The king had refused his request, and now the men of Israel had lost confidence in him as a leader. He prayed to the Lord in anguish, "Since I came to Pharaoh to speak in Your name, he has done evil to this

people; neither have You delivered Your people at all." Then Moses received a wonderful promise. God said to him, "Say to the children of Israel: 'I am the Lord; I will bring you out from under the burdens of the Egyptians, I will rescue you from their bondage, and I will redeem you with an outstretched arm and with great judgments. I will take you as My people, and I will be your God. Then you shall know that I am the Lord your God who brings you out from under the burdens of the Egyptians.' "

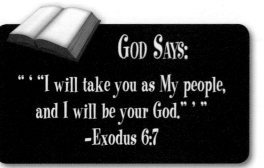

GOD SAYS:

" ' "I will take you as My people, and I will be your God." ' "
-Exodus 6:7

Pharaoh had said the people could not go, but the Lord promised that they would be delivered. The stage was set for a power contest between the will of the king of Egypt and the will of the God of heaven.

Following the Lord's instructions, Moses and Aaron made their way to the bank of the Nile River one morning to meet Pharaoh, who went there each day to bathe and to worship the river god. Moses told Pharaoh that because he had disobeyed the Lord by refusing to let the children of Israel go, a plague would come upon that land. In the presence of the king and his courtiers, Moses stretched out his staff and struck the water, and right before their eyes the Nile River turned to blood. This was a disaster to the Egyptians because they worshiped the river. The fish began to die, and the river became so smelly and polluted that people could get no water to drink. They tried digging shallow wells near the riverbank, but then the water in buckets and stone jars turned to blood.

For seven days this plague lasted, but Pharaoh persisted in his refusal to allow the Israelites to go.

Then came slimy frogs swarming over the land, hopping into houses, into beds, into kitchens, and into dishes of food. The Egyptians would not destroy the frogs because they looked upon them as sacred. The pests took possession of everything, even the king's palace. Pharaoh told Moses and Aaron that he would allow the people to leave if the frogs were removed. But when all the frogs died, the king refused to fulfill his promise.

The third plague made the Egyptians completely miserable. The dust on the ground turned to lice. The tiny vermin crawled on the clothes, on the bodies, and in the hair of the people. Then, after that, the air was filled with clouds of flies, and the land was ruined by them. In spite of these calamities, Pharaoh still refused to free the Israelites.

The next plague was a disease that struck the cows, donkeys, horses, and camels. Although the Egyptians lost much of their livestock to the deadly disease, none of the animals belonging to the people of Israel were touched by it.

The sixth plague brought terrible suffering. Boils and sores broke out on the skin of both the people and the remaining animals, and loud cries of pain went up throughout the land. But none of the Israelites got boils or sores. As each plague had come to the people of Egypt, Pharaoh

QUICK FACT:
God proved through the plagues that He is the only God and that Pharaoh was powerless to protect his people.

had repented and told Moses to take the Israelites to the desert. But after the plagues went away, he hardened his heart and refused to let them go.

Then "the Lord sent thunder and hail, and [lightning] darted to the ground." The hail destroyed cows in the field, and it broke down the barley and flax crops. It tore branches from trees and stripped them of their leaves. Egypt was a desert land where it seldom rained or hailed, and this severe storm was "so very heavy that there was none like it in all the land of Egypt since it became a nation." The land of Goshen, however, had no storm or hail at all. Pharaoh begged Moses to call on God to stop the storm and he would free the Hebrews. When Moses spread his arms toward the storm, it quickly ceased. But again Pharaoh changed his mind, because he still did not believe in the authority of God in heaven.

A plague of locusts followed the storm. Great swarms of these insects covered the ground. The grain in the fields and the leaves on the trees that had not been ruined by the hail were eaten by the hungry horde. However, after the locusts had eaten every green leaf and were blown away by a strong wind, Pharaoh still refused to allow the Israelites to leave Egypt.

The country was bare and desolate when the next plague struck—a plague of deep darkness. For three days it was so dark that the people could not see one another nor find their way around. But in homes of the Israelites there was light.

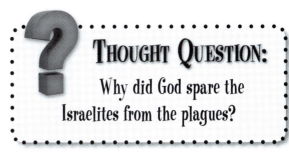

THOUGHT QUESTION:
Why did God spare the Israelites from the plagues?

Now Pharaoh summoned Moses and said, "Go, serve the Lord; only let your flocks and your herds be kept back. Let your little ones also go with you."

The shrewd ruler knew that if the people went away without their cattle and sheep, they would be forced to return to Egypt. They could not make a long journey without them.

Moses refused this offer, standing firm by his request that his people go with all their livestock and other possessions. In great anger Pharaoh shouted, "Get away from me! Take heed to yourself and see my face no more! For in the day you see my face you shall die!"

"You have spoken well," said Moses. "I will never see your face again."

One more plague would fall on the wicked nation. It would bring more terrible results than all the nine plagues that had already punished Egypt.

THE LAST NIGHT IN EGYPT

Exodus 11–14:14

A s the plagues fell one by one on the land of Egypt, the children of Israel, protected by the power of God, watched with amazement from their houses. They saw great catastrophes come upon the proud nation in the form of infestation, disease, storm, and darkness; they saw the Egyptians humbled by these horrible punishments.

One day Moses announced to the Israelites that God was ready to deliver His people. Following the instruction of their leaders, the people made secret preparations for their journey. They asked for and received presents from the Egyptians, gifts of gold and silver as well as jewels and clothing. The Spirit of God influenced the Egyptians to give generously to the people who had been their slaves.

As the sun set that evening, every family in Goshen prepared a special dinner. The father killed a lamb; and while the mother prepared and roasted it, the father took some of the animal's blood and smeared it on the doorposts and on the lintel over the door with a bunch of the herb called hyssop. As the children watched this strange ceremony, they must have asked the meaning of it. The father told them it was a sign on the house so the Lord would "pass over" it and spare the family from the last terrible plague that would come to Egypt that night.

When darkness came, the streets of Goshen were empty because the Israelites stayed in their houses as Moses had commanded. It was the hour for each family to participate in the Passover Feast. The father and mother gathered their children around the table. As they stood, dressed and ready for the journey into the desert, they ate the roast lamb, bitter herbs, and bread made without yeast.

GOD SAYS:
" ' "So this day shall be to you a memorial; and you shall keep it as a feast to the Lord throughout your generations." ' " –Exodus 12:14

In this way the Israelites celebrated the first Passover supper. To commemorate their deliverance, they were to observe the Passover Feast every year because God said, " 'This day shall be to you a memorial; and you shall keep it as a feast to the Lord throughout your generations. You shall keep it as a feast by an everlasting ordinance.' " That is the reason the Jews observe the Passover supper to this day. It is a vivid reminder to them of how God spared Israel and brought the people out of slavery.

Just as the pioneers of old—Adam, Abraham, Isaac, and Jacob—had offered sacrifices to help them remember the promise of a coming Savior, so this Passover lamb pointed toward the time when Jesus, "the Lamb of God," would die to save people from the death curse of sin. They ate unleavened bread because of the hurried departure the

Israelites had to make in order to leave Egypt, giving them no time to bake bread with yeast. And the meal included bitter herbs to remind the people of the bitter years they had suffered in Egypt.

When midnight came, a terrible cry of mourning rose up in the land of Egypt. From Pharaoh's palace to the humblest little house, there was weeping for the dead. The eldest child in every family, "from the firstborn of Pharaoh who sat on his throne to the firstborn of the captive who was in the dungeon, and all the firstborn of livestock" was struck down by the angel of death. But the families of Israel were saved, as long as the blood of a lamb had been spread on the door of their home.

Messengers from the palace hurried through the darkness to find Moses and Aaron. When the brothers appeared

before Pharaoh, he spoke in a trembling voice: "Rise and go out from among my people," he said, "both you and the children of Israel. And go, serve the Lord as you have said. Also take your flocks and your herds, as you have said, and be gone; and bless me also."

At last the haughty monarch was willing to bow to God's plan.

He knew that all the plagues had come upon his people because of his stubborn refusal to obey the Lord.

The word immediately went to every family in Israel to start on the journey. The people left their houses so quickly

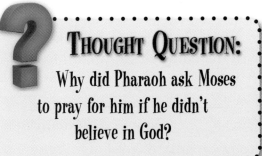

THOUGHT QUESTION:

Why did Pharaoh ask Moses to pray for him if he didn't believe in God?

that the women had to snatch up the dough from the bread troughs without baking it into bread. With great excitement, men and women, boys and girls, hurried down the road in the darkness. Donkeys, camels, flocks of sheep, and herds of cattle were driven from the pastures.

In all the hurrying and noise, Moses did not overlook one important duty. He commanded that some men carry the coffin containing the mummy of Joseph. It was Joseph's wish to be buried in Canaan, the land of his birth. Almost 150 years earlier, Joseph had said, "God will surely visit you, and you shall carry up my bones from here." The faith of this great pioneer was rewarded. His people were now going back to the homeland God had promised them.

Six hundred thousand men, besides the women and children, marched out of Egypt in orderly groups. With them went huge herds of animals, which had greatly increased during the long stay in Goshen. Many Egyptians went along with them, because they had seen how the God of heaven protected and prospered Israel, and they wanted to share in the blessings.

From the first day of the Exodus out of Egypt, God stayed near the Israelites in a cloud that led them in the daytime and a pillar of fire that gave them light at night. The cloud led the great caravan south along the edge of the desert for several days until it came to the shores of the Red Sea. While the people were resting there, they looked back and saw, far behind them, a great cloud of dust. As they watched, they began to see the afternoon sunlight gleaming on chariots and on the armor of advancing soldiers.

The army of Pharaoh was coming after them. There was no way to escape because mountains loomed on the right and on the left, and in front of them was the Red Sea. Angry voices cried out against Moses, saying, "Because there were no graves in Egypt, have you taken us away to die in the wilderness? Why have you so dealt with us, to bring us up out of Egypt?" How quickly the children of Israel forgot God's promises!

Moses, a strong and patient man, listened to the cries of the frightened people. In that moment courage came to his heart, because he knew that God would save them. "Do not be afraid. Stand still, and see the salvation of the Lord, which He will accomplish for you to-

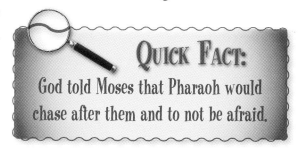

QUICK FACT:
God told Moses that Pharaoh would chase after them and to not be afraid.

day," he said boldly. Then he added, "The Lord will fight for you, and you shall hold your peace."

But the sun had set, and darkness now fell on the vast crowd of terror-stricken campers. The pillar of cloud moved between the Israelite multitude and the enemy army, hiding the Israelites from their pursuers. That evening, Moses stretched out his hand over the Red Sea, and a wonderful thing happened during the night!

WATER FROM THE ROCK

Exodus 14–17:8

The morning after the last plague had struck the land of the Nile, the Egyptians faced a dismal sight. Their country had been ruined by hail and storm; most of their farm animals had been killed; and now they were going into mourning and preparing for a funeral of the firstborn in every home.

But when the dead had been buried, the people began to miss their slaves and wished they had them back to do their work. Then Pharaoh received word from his messengers that the children of Israel were marching farther and farther from Egypt. If he did not act at once, they would escape from his clutches forever.

The king called his chief officers together. When they heard the news, their hearts turned against the people of God. They said, "Why have we done this, that we have let Israel go from serving us?"

Pharaoh summoned his generals, and they quickly marshaled foot soldiers, cavalry, and six hundred chariots. Shouts and commands echoed across the fields as the army started in pursuit of the vulnerable Israelites.

In the afternoon Pharaoh gave a shout of triumph as he rode ahead of the army in his royal chariot. He could see that by the shores of the Red Sea was the large camp of the Hebrews. *Soon we will have our slaves again,* he thought.

However, as the chariots and cavalry came near the camp, an angel moved in front of them. The pillar of cloud, which was usually at the front of the Israelite caravan, moved around behind them. The army stopped, not daring to ride through what looked to them like a thick, dark cloud. So, the command rang out for the soldiers to make camp for the night.

That evening Moses stretched out his arm over the Red Sea, and the Lord caused a strong east wind to blow all night. The waters of the sea were divided, and they formed a wall on the right and on the left. Between them there was dry seabed. In the early morning darkness, the Israelites got

GOD SAYS:

" 'Do not be afraid. Stand still, and see the salvation of the Lord, which He will accomplish for you today.' " -Exodus 14:13

ready to move and marched across the Red Sea, the first ones reaching the farther shore before the sun came up.

The Egyptian guards gave the alarm as soon as they could see what was happening. The slaves were escaping through a path in the sea! At the sound of trumpets, the soldiers on horseback and in chariots rushed into the seabed. God was watching and made chariots lose their wheels. The heavy vehicles bogged down in the soft ground, and although the horses pulled and strained, they could not move ahead.

As the sun rose, Moses saw the Egyptian army stalled in the bed of the sea. He put out his hand over the water and giant waves were unleashed, covering the chariots and soldiers. The army of Pharaoh was swept away and destroyed.

Here was complete victory for the Israelites! A thrill of happiness came over the tired travelers as they watched their enemies defeated before their eyes. They would never need to return to Egypt as slaves.

Moses led the whole assembly in a song of victory, while his sister Miriam picked up a tambourine and all the women of the camp followed her, playing on their tambourines and dancing. They sang this song and praised the Lord who had saved them:

"I will sing to the Lord,
For He has triumphed gloriously!

The horse and its rider
He has thrown into the sea!
The Lord is my strength and song,
And He has become my salvation;
He is my God, and I will praise Him;
My father's God, and I will exalt Him.

Pharaoh's chariots and his army He has cast
    into the sea;
His chosen captains also are drowned in the
    Red Sea.
The depths have covered them;
They sank to the bottom like a stone."

Leaving the Red Sea, the Israelites trekked through the desert of Shur. For a while they forgot the heat of the sun and the dry, burning sand. They were happy to be free from their slave masters, and they thanked God for bringing them victory. Special protection was given to them on their journey. The great cloud hovered over the caravan during the day to shelter it from the fierce heat, and the cloud of

QUICK FACT:
The cloud protected the Israelites from the heat of the desert during the day, and the fire gave them light at night and kept them warm in the cool night air.

fire hovered above the camp at night to give light. When they moved on, the people knew where to go because the pillar of cloud always moved ahead of them, directing their way.

For three days the men, women, and children marched. They found no streams in the desert, but they did not worry, because they carried fresh water in canteens made from the skins of animals. In that dry country, however, they soon used up their supply, and then they began to whine and complain. Moses, who had traveled through the wilderness, knew that they were approaching Marah, where there were springs of water; but his heart sank as he remembered that the water from those springs was bitter.

A shout of relief went up from the people when they saw the water of the springs pouring over the rocks. When the crowds of men, women, and children ran forward to get a drink, they cried out in disappointment because the water tasted bad and was unfit to drink. Then the multitude turned on Moses, saying, "What shall we drink?"

The Lord showed Moses a tree and directed him to throw it into the water. This done, the bitter water became sweet. Then everyone came to the springs to drink.

While the Israelites rested, Moses talked to them about obeying God and following His commands. There were some in the camp who wanted to do as they pleased. If they refused to obey the rules, they would have trouble and sorrow; but if they willingly obeyed the Lord's commands, He would protect them and bring them safely to their new home in Canaan.

The next stop of their journey was Elim, where there were twelve springs of water and seventy palm trees. Soon the pillar of cloud moved ahead, and the Israelites took up the march again. By this time the people had been on the road for more than a month. Their supply of food was low, and as they looked across the rough, barren country, they knew they would not find anything to eat in this wasteland. Again they began to complain, and soon they came to Moses and Aaron with their troubles.

"Oh, that we had died by the hand of the Lord in the land of Egypt, when we sat by the pots of meat and when we ate bread to the full!" the Israelites said to them. "For you have brought us out into this wilderness to kill this whole assembly with hunger."

Poor Moses. He had helped the people gain their freedom, but now they wanted to be back in Egypt as slaves!

He might have scolded them, but he was patient. Again he turned to God for help, and the Lord promised food for the hungry multitude.

That evening, flocks of quail flew into the camp, and there were enough to supply the people with dinner. The next morning when the Israelites woke up, they found the ground covered with white objects that looked like small, round seeds, as thin as frost.

"What is it?" they asked.

Moses told them that this was the bread God was giving them from heaven. It would appear six mornings through the week, he said, and each family should gather its share. On the sixth day they were to gather twice as much, because none of the food would appear on the seventh day, the Sabbath.

THOUGHT QUESTION:

Why wasn't there any manna on the ground on the Sabbath?

Fathers and mothers and kids picked up the strange seedlike food. They called it manna, which means "what is it?" They ground it into flour and made cakes and baked them. It tasted like wafers made with honey.

The people were told to gather just enough manna for one day, but some were greedy. They did not believe it would come every day, so they gathered extra. It turned out to be a bad idea for the greedy ones to hoard the manna, because the next morning it smelled bad and had worms in it. Yet, when the people picked up a double supply on Friday for the Sabbath, as God had instructed them, the manna remained fresh and good to eat for both days.

The caravan moved onward and came to Rephidim, a dry, rocky spot in the desert. Here there was no water, and again the people complained to Moses, shouting, "Give us water, that we may drink."

In his distress Moses cried to the Lord, "What shall I do with this people?" And God told Moses exactly what he should do.

The patient leader took some of the chief men with him to the hot, bare rocks of Horeb. The thirsty people watched. Did Moses think he could get water out of those scorching hot rocks? What were these men going to do? Carrying his shepherd's rod, Moses walked up to the rocks. He thought of the days when he had herded sheep in this desert and remembered God's promise at the burning bush. He lifted his rod—the one he had used to turn the water of the Nile into blood—and struck a blow. Instantly a torrent of cold, sparkling water gushed out and flowed down the slope, and the waiting people rushed forward to drink.

But there was happiness for only a short time. Soon scouts came hurrying to Moses with bad news: a fierce tribe from the desert was coming to attack Israel. The Amalekites, cruel, savage warriors, were already overtaking some of the stragglers who had become separated from the main caravan of Israelites. Moses knew that his people were not ready for a battle. They had been slaves, not soldiers. But the military training of Egypt came back to Moses, and he commanded his men to prepare to fight anyway. He would give them hurried instruction in warfare and send them to defeat the enemy before the camp of Israel was assaulted.

WHEN GOD SPOKE FROM THE MOUNTAIN

Exodus 17:10–32:2

Moses picked a man named Joshua to command the army of Israel. He was young and courageous, a leader who could be trusted. When the news came that the warriors of Chief Amalek were coming to attack the camp, Moses gave this instruction to Joshua: "Choose us some men and go out, fight with Amalek. Tomorrow I will stand on the top of the hill with the rod of God in my hand."

Joshua gathered young men who could fight, and he gave them weapons. They were probably equipped with swords and spears or javelins, such as the Egyptians used. When the soldiers had been quickly instructed, Joshua led them into the desert to find the Amalekites.

While the army of Israel advanced, Moses, Aaron, and Hur climbed the hill to watch the

45

combat. Soon the two armies clashed in battle. Whenever Moses help up his hand, Joshua and his band of warriors were able to win. When Moses let his hand down, the Amalekites would advance. After a while Moses' arms got tired, so Aaron and Hur had him sit on a large, flat rock while they stood beside him and held up his hands. At sunset the army of Israel was victorious.

It was while the caravan was camped near Rephidim that Moses was surprised and happy to see visitors coming toward his tent: his wife, Zipporah, his two sons, Gershom and Eliezer, and Jethro, his father-in-law. Jethro, who lived in the desert, had heard of the wonderful deliverance of Israel from Egypt. He was anxious to see the nation on the march toward the land of Canaan. Moses greeted his family and told them how God had saved the nation at the Red Sea.

> **GOD SAYS:**
>
> "And so it was, when Moses held up his hand, that Israel prevailed; and when he let down his hand, Amalek prevailed." -Exodus 17:11

The next day Jethro watched Moses hold court for the camp. All day long, the patient leader listened to requests and complaints.

"What is this thing that you are doing for the people? Why do you alone sit, and all the people stand before you from morning until evening?" Jethro asked.

"Because the people come to me to inquire of God," Moses said to his father-in-law.

"The thing that you do is not good," Jethro said to him. "Both you and these people who are here with you will surely wear yourselves out. For this thing is too much for you; you are not able to perform it by yourself."

Then Jethro advised Moses to adopt a new plan of organization. Captains would be given charge over groups of thousands, hundreds, fifties, and tens. These men were to act as judges in all the smaller matters. Only the most serious difficulties should be brought to Moses. The plan seemed good to Moses, and he chose wise men to assist him. When Jethro saw that the plan was working well, he said Goodbye to Moses and departed for his home in Midian.

About three months after leaving the land of Egypt, the caravan of Israel, with wagons, flocks, and herds, came to the plains near Mount Sinai. This made an ideal campsite for the thousands and thousands of people, where they could rest after days of marching. Above them towered the rugged mountain peaks. By day the pillar of cloud hovered over the camp, and at night the cloud of fire gave protection. While the people slept, the manna, or bread from heaven, fell gently to the ground in the camp.

The boys and girls must have had a lot of fun. They helped pack and unpack when the caravan moved. They could gather the

THOUGHT QUESTION:
Why was Moses' job too hard for him to handle alone?

manna, bring wood for fires, and carry water for cooking and washing. When they were free to play, they could go for hikes in the hills and watch the wild creatures. Near the mountains were meadows, where trees and wild flowers grew.

Soon after the nation had settled on the plain, Moses was commanded to climb the steep, rocky trail up the side of Mount Sinai to receive a message from God. The Lord told Moses that if the people would be obedient, they would be a precious treasure to Him. When Moses came down from the mountain and told the people what God had commanded, they answered, "All that the Lord has spoken we will do."

Then came some exciting news. The Israelites were to prepare for a very special occasion. They were to wash themselves and their clothes and stand ready, because God was going to speak to the nation from the summit of the mountain.

On the third day the men, women, and children looked toward Mount Sinai. The top was covered with a thick, black cloud that swept down until it encircled the entire mountain. At that moment one of Moses' assistants sounded a trumpet, and the people marched forward to the base of the mountain. From the cloud lightning flashed, followed by thunder crashes that echoed across the plain. The people were frightened and fell to the ground. Even Moses trembled.

Then there was silence. A hush fell on the vast multitude. The voice of God was heard. In this solemn setting He spoke the Ten Commandments so that every man and woman and boy and girl could hear.

When God had finished speaking, the frightened people moved back from the mountain. "Do not fear," said Moses to the people, "for God has come to test you, and that His fear may be before you, so that you may not sin."

Once more Moses was commanded to climb to the summit of Mount Sinai, and this time he took Joshua, the leader of the army, with him. Aaron, the brother of Moses, and Hur were left in charge of the camp. Each day the people watched for their leader to return. Weeks passed, and finally they said impatiently, "We do not know what has become of him."

QUICK FACT:

Moses acted as a go-between, a mediator. He spoke to God for the Israelites, and relayed God's will to them.

The camp grew more and more restless. The people wanted to have a good time. When Moses had been gone almost forty days, some of the Israelites came to Aaron with a plan. Aaron listened to the grumbling crowd that had already forgotten God. Then he made a terrible mistake that led to the death of thousands of Israelites.

REBELLION IN THE CAMP

Exodus 32–35:20

When the children of Israel had gathered around Aaron, they began shouting, "Come, make us gods that shall go before us; for as for this Moses, the man who brought us up out of the land of Egypt, we do not know what has become of him." Aaron, who was in charge of the camp while his brother was away, should have stood up for what was right. But he was afraid of the impatient crowd, so he said, "Break off the golden earrings which are in the ears of your wives, your sons, and your daughters, and bring them to me." The people did as he asked. They had many ornaments of gold that they had brought from Egypt.

Taking the trinkets, Aaron threw them into a pot and melted the gold. Then he poured the metal into a mold and made an idol in the shape of a calf. The Israelites were happy when they saw this golden image. The cow was one of the gods of the land of the Nile that the Israelites had seen the Egyptians worshiping many times.

"This is your god, O Israel, that brought you out of the land of Egypt!" shouted the people as they bowed before the idol. When Aaron saw this demonstration, he commanded that an altar be built in front of the golden image. He said, "Tomorrow is a feast to the Lord."

So, the next morning the people gathered in front of the golden calf to offer sacrifices and to dance. Afterward they sat down to eat and drink and then got up to play.

While this was happening, Moses was talking with God on the mountain. The leader had received the Ten Commandments

engraved by the finger of God on two tablets of stone. He did not know what was taking place among the people until God, who sees all that people do, told him about the terrible sin going on below. The Lord gave this command to Moses: "Go, get down! For your people whom you brought out of the land of Egypt have corrupted themselves. They have turned aside quickly out of the way which I commanded them." God said that He wished to destroy the children of Israel and make a new nation from Moses' own family. But Moses pleaded for the lives of his people, saying, "Remember Abraham, Isaac, and Israel, Your servants, to whom You swore by Your own self, and said to them, 'I will multiply your descendants as the stars of heaven; and all this land that I have spoken of I give to your descendants, and they shall inherit it forever.'" So, the Lord changed His mind and did not harm the people.

Holding the sacred stone tablets with great care, Moses made his way down the mountain trail. Joshua guided the steps of the aging leader along the rough pathway. Once, the two men stopped where they could see the camp spread out over the broad plain. Joshua heard noise coming from the Israelites,

and he said, "There is a noise of war in the camp." As the leader of the army, he was afraid that an enemy had attacked his people. But Moses replied,

"It is not the noise of the shout of victory,
Nor the noise of the cry of defeat,
But the sound of singing I hear."

The two men rushed ahead quickly. Soon they came in full view of the camp of Israel. When Moses saw the people dancing and singing around the golden idol, he could scarcely believe his eyes. As he came near the crowd, he threw the tablets of the Ten Commandments to the ground, where they smashed to bits. When the people saw what Moses had done, they stopped singing and dancing. With anger in his eyes, Moses marched forward and seized the golden idol. Before anyone dared to protest, he threw it into the fire. He had the gold ground into powder and thrown into the water. Then he commanded the people to drink it. In this way he tried to impress upon the multitude the worthlessness of the idol they had worshiped.

QUICK FACT:
Moses was gone forty days, and the Israelites didn't think he was coming back. So they asked Aaron to make them a golden calf to worship.

Moses called his brother, Aaron, to him and asked, "What did this people do to you that you have brought so great a sin upon them?"

Aaron tried to excuse himself by saying that the people had forced him to carry out their wishes. He went on to say that he had thrown the gold into the fire, and, voilà, this golden calf had come out!

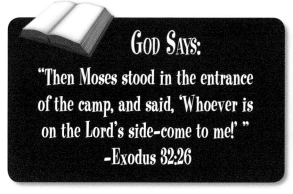

GOD SAYS: "Then Moses stood in the entrance of the camp, and said, 'Whoever is on the Lord's side-come to me!' " -Exodus 32:26

Moses knew that the people had rebelled against God, whom they had promised to serve faithfully. Because God's law had been broken, Moses knew that the guilty must be punished. The entire camp had heard God's commandments, and the first and second rules said, "You shall have no other gods before Me. You shall not make for yourself any carved image, or any likeness of anything that is in heaven above, or that is in the earth beneath, or that is in the water under the earth; you shall not bow down to them nor serve them."

Standing in the main entrance of the camp, Moses shouted for all the people who were on God's side to join him. The people of the tribe of Levi gathered around him. Moses told them to kill men in the camp as a lesson to the whole nation that if they rebelled against God, they themselves were betraying their family and friends. As a result of their rebellion, three thousand men were killed by the sword that day.

The next morning Moses said to the people, "You have committed a great sin. So now I will go up to the Lord; perhaps I can make atonement for your sin." The humble leader loved the children of Israel. He had given up the honors of the royal palace of Egypt to lead them out of slavery. He had prayed to the Lord many times for their protection, but now he must kneel and plead that the nation be saved from destruction.

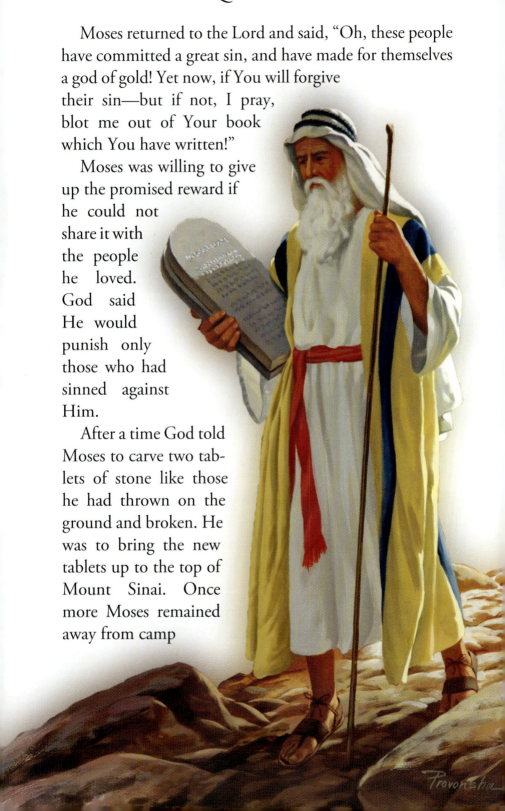

Moses returned to the Lord and said, "Oh, these people have committed a great sin, and have made for themselves a god of gold! Yet now, if You will forgive their sin—but if not, I pray, blot me out of Your book which You have written!"

Moses was willing to give up the promised reward if he could not share it with the people he loved. God said He would punish only those who had sinned against Him.

After a time God told Moses to carve two tablets of stone like those he had thrown on the ground and broken. He was to bring the new tablets up to the top of Mount Sinai. Once more Moses remained away from camp for forty days, and during this time the Ten Command-ments engraved in stone were given to him a second time.

When Moses descended from the mountain with the law in his hands, his face glowed, because he had been in the presence of the Lord. The people in camp saw the glow on his face and were afraid. When the leader spoke to the Israelites, he put a veil over his face.

Moses told the con-gregation of the plan to build a tent of meet-ing, a sanctuary, where all the people could worship the God of heaven. He asked everyone to bring gifts for this house of worship.

THOUGHT QUESTION:
Why was it important that people be punished for worshiping an idol?

GOD MEETS WITH HIS PEOPLE

Exodus 35:21–40

A feeling of excitement began to rise in the camp of the Israelites. Women were opening little boxes and leather bags in which they kept their gold pins, rings, and necklaces. They were searching for the most valuable jewels they possessed. Some of their ornaments had gone to make the shameful golden idol, but now they were giving their treasures for a tent of meeting—a place where God would live with His people.

Many of the men were sorting the skins of goats and rams. Only the best of these would be gifts for the Lord. Each morning the people came to Moses with their offerings. Women brought brooches, earrings, necklaces, and other gold objects, while the men came loaded with fine linen cloth, goat hair, and ram skins. Boys must have carried pieces of acacia wood for the construction, while the girls brought jars of spices and incense for the burnt offerings.

Bezaleel and Aholiab were the two men chosen to direct the construction of the tent of meeting. They had charge of the weaving, the metalwork, and the wood carving. Soon there was so much material on hand that the leaders said to Moses, "The people bring much more than enough for the service of the work which the Lord commanded us to do." So, Moses issued an order that was proclaimed throughout the camp: "Let neither man nor woman do any more work for the offering of the sanctuary."

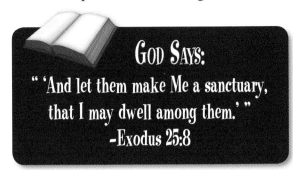

GOD SAYS:

" 'And let them make Me a sanctuary, that I may dwell among them.' "
–Exodus 25:8

All the skilled workers were set to the tasks of spinning yarn, weaving cloth, sewing the curtains, and embroidering them. Men who were skillful with the needle sewed the rams' skins together for the outer covering of the sanctuary. Others built the wooden frames and made the metal pedestals that would hold the building in place. Bezaleel constructed the beautiful gold-covered furniture for the tent of meeting; he also made the gold and bronze utensils to be used in the sanctuary services.

The day came when the work on the tent of meeting was finished. The tent was about eighteen feet wide and fifty-five feet long. Moses inspected the curtains, the gold-covered boards for the walls, the metal pedestals and pillars, and the magnificent furniture. He spoke his blessing on the workers for their faithful service.

Then the workers set up the tent of meeting in the middle of the camp. They hung the curtains on all sides around the tent to form a courtyard. The roof was made of four sets of curtains. The inner drapery was of fine linen, on which were embroidered figures of angels. Over this was placed a covering of woven goats' hair, a third covering was of rams' skins, and the outside covering was badgers' skins. Thick boards plated with pure gold were set on the side to form the walls. These boards were placed in silver sockets and held in their proper position with pillars and bars.

The tent of meeting had two rooms separated by a beautiful curtain. The inner room was called the Holy of Holies; the outer room, the Holy Place. The outer chamber had three beautiful pieces of furniture: a golden table, a richly carved golden candlestick, and a golden altar of incense. On the golden table, twelve loaves of fresh bread were placed each Sabbath morning, one for each of the twelve tribes of Israel. The golden candlestick had seven oil lamps that were kept burning continually. In front of the curtain separating the two rooms was the golden altar on which incense was burned morning and evening. In the smaller room, the Holy of Holies, was the ark of the covenant. This beautiful chest was covered with pure gold on the outside and on the inside. The cover of this chest was a solid piece of gold called the mercy seat. On this mercy seat were two angel figures called cherubim, formed from pieces of pure gold. Their wings were spread out to overshadow the mercy seat; their faces were turned toward each other, and their heads were bowed in reverence.

QUICK FACT:
While up on Mount Sinai, God showed Moses a picture of the heavenly sanctuary, and gave him instructions on how to make one just like it.

The two tablets of stone on which the Ten Commandments were engraved were placed inside the ark. A golden pot containing manna was also kept in the ark. Above the mercy seat, between the golden angels, rested a glorious light, the sign that God was meeting with His people.

The tent of meeting was not a church for all the people to enter. It was a tabernacle, a holy place where only specially chosen priests could minister before the Lord. Because the tribe of Levi had not worshiped the golden idol, Moses selected the men from this tribe to be the

Lars Justinen

priests in the tabernacle. The priests who conducted the regular service in the Holy Place wore white robes made of fine linen cloth; but for Aaron, the first man to be the high priest, there was a beautiful blue robe to wear over his white one. On the hem of the blue garment were embroidered pomegranates, and between these hung tiny golden bells. The high priest also wore an ephod, a short sleeveless garment somewhat like a vest jacket.

The high priest wore a beautiful breastplate, which was considered very sacred. It was made of a piece of linen cloth, embroidered in gold and set with twelve precious gems. On each gem was the name of one of the tribes. In addition to these twelve stones, the priest wore two other gems, called the Urim and the Thummim, by which God made known His will to the people. The high priest was the only one who entered the Holy of Holies. He ministered there once each year.

When the tent of meeting had been set up and all was ready, Aaron and his four sons were dedicated as priests. Then a cloud covered the tent of meeting, while the glory of the Lord filled the sanctuary. In this way God revealed to His people that He was pleased with the place of worship they had prepared for Him.

THOUGHT QUESTION:

Why was the high priest the only one allowed to enter the Holy of Holies?

The cloud hovered over the tabernacle by day and became the pillar of fire by night. When the cloud rose high above the sanctuary, the people knew it was time for them to move forward on their journey to the Promised Land.

TRAGEDY AT THE BORDER

Numbers 10:11–14:45

O ne morning, after the children of Israel had camped in the plain below Mount Sinai for about fourteen months, the cloud rose up from the tent of meeting and moved forward. News passed quickly from tent to tent throughout the camp. "We are moving! We are moving!"

Men of the tribe of Levi who had been assigned to the task took down the tent of meeting in sections and carried it. Priests carried the ark with poles that were put through rings on the sides of the chest. The other pieces of golden furniture were carried in the same way.

The children of Israel journeyed until they came to the wilderness of Paran, south and west of the land of Canaan. Eleven days after they left Mount Sinai, Moses gave the signal to make a permanent camp, because the cloud had stopped over Kadesh.

Now the fears and troubles of the desert had passed. Kadesh was a beautiful oasis near the border of Canaan. Grass covered the valley, and streams of water flowed from among the rocks. Trees laden with sweet fruit were a promise of the good things the people would have when they entered Canaan.

It was time to make plans to enter the land. Moses chose twelve men, one from each tribe, and sent them to spy out the country, to check on the local people and their strength. Before they started on their dangerous task, he gave instructions to the men, saying, "Go up this way into the South, and go up to the mountains, and see what the land is like: whether the people who dwell in it are strong or weak, few or many; whether the land they dwell in is good or bad; whether the cities they inhabit are like camps or strongholds; whether the land is rich or poor; and whether there are forests there or not. Be of good courage. And bring some of the fruit of the land."

The men were gone almost six weeks. The Israelites must have gathered in groups and talked about the country they were going to conquer. They waited day after day for the spies to return. One evening a shout echoed through the camp. "The spies have returned. Now we can go into our Promised Land!" people said one to an-

other. The twelve men came before Moses and Aaron, bearing the fruit they had gathered. Two of them carried a giant cluster of grapes on a pole between them, while others brought in baskets of figs and pomegranates. Moses waited anxiously for the report of the spies' strange adventure.

"We went to the land where you sent us," one of the spies began. "It truly flows with milk and honey, and this is its fruit." A murmur of happiness must have swept through the crowd as the people heard the words of the spies and saw the fruit of the land. But then the men said, "Nevertheless the people who dwell in the land are strong; the cities are fortified and very large; moreover we saw the descendants of Anak [giants] there."

A wail of terror came from the listening multitude. Men scowled, and women began to weep. Then Caleb, one of the spies, quieted the crowd and said in a loud voice, "Let us go up at once and take possession, for we are well able to overcome it." Joshua, the warrior, joined Caleb in his challenge to go forward. These two men were not afraid to conquer the enemy. They knew that God had promised to be with Israel as they marched.

But the other ten spies cried out, "We are not able to go up against the people, for they are stronger than we."

All that night the people were groaning in the camp.

3—C. H.

The dreams and hopes of the hundred of thousands of people had been shattered. They were ready to rebel against Moses and pick someone to take them back to Egypt.

The next morning the Israelites continued to grumble against Moses and Aaron. "If only we had died in the land of Egypt!" the whole community said to them. "Or if only we had died in this wilderness!" Others said, "Let us select a leader and return to Egypt."

Moses and Aaron were very sad because the people had rebelled against the command of God.

GOD SAYS:

" 'If the Lord delights in us, then He will bring us into this land and give it to us, "a land which flows with milk and honey." ' " -Numbers 14:8

Once more Caleb and Joshua stood up before the mob and spoke with courage. They said, "The land we passed through to spy out is an exceedingly good land. If the Lord delights in us, then He will bring us into this land and give it to us, 'a land which flows with milk and honey.' Only do not rebel against the Lord, nor fear the people of the land, for they are our bread; their protection has departed from them, and the Lord is with us. Do not fear them." But the people refused to listen. In their insane rage they picked up stones and rushed at the two men to kill them.

But the evil, rebellious crowd stopped suddenly. The stones dropped from their hands. "Look at the tent of meeting!" someone shouted. The glory of the Lord, like a flame of fire, suddenly appeared over the tent of meeting. With fear and trembling the people bowed their heads.

The Lord said to Moses, "How long shall I bear with this evil congregation who murmur against Me? I have heard the murmurings which the children of Israel murmur against Me. Say to them, 'As I live,' says the Lord, 'just as you have spoken in My hearing, so I will do to you: The carcasses of you who have murmured against Me shall fall in this wilderness, all of you who were numbered, according to your entire number, from twenty years old and above. Except for Caleb the son of Jephunneh and Joshua the son of Nun, you shall by no means enter the land which I swore I would make you dwell in.' " What a terrible fate for all the Israelites who were more than twenty years old! They were doomed to wander in the wilderness and die there because they rebelled against God's word. Of the older generation only Joshua and Caleb would go through to the Promised Land. With these two faithful men, the children and the young people who had not taken part in the rebellion would possess the land.

When Moses told the nation what its punishment would be, the people were brokenhearted and cried. The next morning they decided to prove that they had courage after all, and they said, "Here we are, and we will go up to the place which the Lord has promised, for we have sinned!"

Moses replied immediately, "Now why do you transgress the command of the Lord?

QUICK FACT:
The Israelites were too scared of the Canaanites to believe God would provide for them.

For this will not succeed. Do not go up, lest you be defeated by your enemies, for the Lord is not among you."

THOUGHT QUESTION:

Why weren't the people allowed to go into the Promised Land?

Once more the people refused to hear instructions, having not learned the lesson of obedience. With swords and spears a band of men rushed to the top of a mountain inside Canaan; but these soldiers were not prepared to fight, and they did not have God's blessing or presence with them. The Canaanites who lived in that region attacked the invaders, and soon the men of Israel were driven back in utter defeat.

It was a sad day when all of Israel packed up the camp and left the green meadows and fruit trees of Kadesh to trudge back into the hot desert. They were haunted by the words they had shouted against Moses and Aaron: "Would that we had died in this desert!" Their own declaration would come true, and they would never see the Promised Land. They would die in the desert because they had refused to go forward at God's command.

THE EARTH SWALLOWS THE REBELS

Numbers 16–20:12

What could the people of Israel do? They had refused to conquer the land God had given them. When they tried to fight the enemy in their own strength, they had been completely defeated. Now there was nothing for them to do but to accept their punishment and live in the desert for the next forty years.

Moses faced problems right away, because the people were bitter with disappointment. Two hundred and fifty of the chief men became jealous of Moses' leadership and wanted to be priests. The leader of the rebels was Korah, a Levite, and he had two assistants named Dathan and Abiram. These men not only defied Moses and the people, but also they refused to obey the commands of God.

Standing before the whole camp, the rebels shouted against Moses and Aaron, saying, "You take too much upon yourselves."

Then Moses declared that on the following day there would be a test in which the Lord would decide who was the leader of Israel. The 250 men who wanted to be priests

69

were to offer incense before the tent of meeting, and God would let the people know who was right.

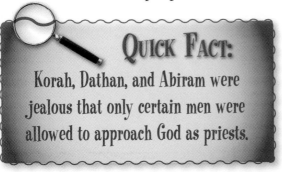

QUICK FACT:

Korah, Dathan, and Abiram were jealous that only certain men were allowed to approach God as priests.

The next morning the rebels appeared, with Korah as their leader. The 250 chiefs brought fire pans and burned incense in front of the tent of meeting. The whole assembly of people had gathered and waited to see what would happen. Suddenly the glory of the Lord appeared over the tent of meeting, and Moses warned the people to move away from the rebels.

Then Moses said loudly, "By this you shall know that the Lord has sent me to do all these works, for I have not done them of my own will. If these men die naturally like all men, . . . then the Lord has not sent me. But if the Lord creates a new thing, and the earth opens its mouth and swallows them up with all that belongs to them, and they go down alive into the pit, then you will understand that these men have rejected the Lord."

As Moses finished speaking, the ground under the three rebel leaders, Korah, Dathan, and Abiram, began to split apart, and a pit in the earth swallowed them and their tents and possessions. Fire came from God and consumed the 250 men who were burning incense in front of the tabernacle. When the people saw this sudden destruction of all the wicked men, they fled from the place in terror.

However, the next day some of the people continued the rebellion, complaining to Moses that he had killed some of God's people the day before. As had happened several times before, God called out to Moses and said that He was ready to destroy the whole nation and start over with Moses' family. Moses then asked Aaron to burn some incense and pray for God's forgiveness and mercy on the children of Israel. God heard the prayer of His priest and did not destroy the whole camp. But a severe plague killed more than fourteen thousand of those who would not obey God.

The nation of Israel moved on. Long, monotonous years in the hot wilderness dragged by. Those who had left Egypt as children were growing up. They were learning to do what their fathers and mothers had not done—obey the Lord's commands. The older generation that could not enter the Promised Land was dying. The whole multitude finally trudged back to Kadesh in the Wilderness of Zin, near Canaan, and there, Moses' sister Miriam died and was buried with great honor. Moses must have mourned the loss of his elder sister, who had cared for him when he was a baby in a basket on the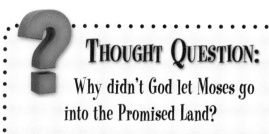

Thought Question: Why didn't God let Moses go into the Promised Land?

Nile and had stayed by his side through the difficult years in the desert.

At last, thirty-eight years of desert travel had passed, and the hills of the Promised Land were in view once more. The people were camped in the same place where water had gushed from the rocks near the beginning of their journey, but now the springs had dried up. As though they had learned nothing from almost forty years in the desert, the people turned against Moses again, saying, "If only we had died when our brethren died before the Lord! Why have you brought up the congregation of the Lord into this wilderness, that we and our animals should die here? . . . It is not a place of grain or figs or vines or pomegranates; nor is there any water to drink."

Moses had struck the rock the first time, but God instructed him on this occasion to take the shepherd's staff and speak to the rock. With Aaron by his side, Moses hurried out to meet the people. "Hear now, you rebels!" he said angrily. "Must we bring water for you out of this rock?"

Raising his hand, Moses struck the rock twice with his staff. The water gushed forth, and the people drank. All

the flocks and herds had water. But in this moment of impatience Moses had disobeyed the Lord. He had taken the glory to himself by saying, "Must we bring water for you," and he had struck the rock when God had instructed him to speak to it.

The Lord said to Moses and Aaron, "Because you did not believe Me, to hallow Me in the eyes of the children of Israel, therefore you shall not bring this congregation into the land which I have given them."

Moses was bitterly disappointed when he heard these words. He would not be the one to lead the people across the Jordan River to their new home. It might seem that he had not committed a great sin. It was only a matter of losing his temper and disobeying God one time. But he and Aaron were the leaders of the people, and this disobedience was enough to keep them from the Promised Land.

> ## GOD SAYS:
> " 'Speak to the rock before their eyes, and it will yield its water; thus you shall bring water for them out of the rock.' " –Numbers 20:8

SERPENTS ENTER THE CAMP

Numbers 20:22–21:9

Aaron is old, and God has told him he will die soon,"
was the message the people in the camp of Israel heard
one day. The nation had moved from Kadesh to Mount
Hor, near Edom, the country of Ishmael's descendants.
God told Moses and Aaron that they should climb Mount
Hor and take Eleazar, the son of Aaron, with them. Eleazar
would take over his father's position of high priest.

All the camp stood watching one morning as Moses,
Aaron, and Eleazar started up the mountain trail. Sometime later the people saw two figures coming down the
side of the mountain. Those with keen eyes said that it was
Moses and Eleazar.

When the people realized that Aaron had died and been
buried on top of the mountain, they mourned his loss for
thirty days. Aaron, the high priest and assistant leader of the
Israelites, had served the nation for almost forty years.

Leaving Mount Hor, the Israelites grew deeply dis-
couraged because the people of Edom would not let them
pass through toward Canaan. They would have to march

around Edom, and they complained to Moses. "Why have you brought us up out of Egypt to die in the wilderness? For there is no food and no water, and our soul loathes this worthless bread." They were no longer grateful for the manna that God provided every day.

It seemed that the people were always complaining. They talked about Egypt, wishing they were once again in the land where they had been slaves. On this occa-

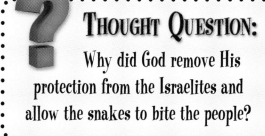

THOUGHT QUESTION: Why did God remove His protection from the Israelites and allow the snakes to bite the people?

sion God took away His protection and allowed the poisonous snakes of the desert to crawl into the tents and bite the people. Terror spread around the camp of Israel. In almost every tent there were dead or dying, because no one was safe from the deadly poison of the snakes. In their great distress the people became humble and repentant. Moses prayed for help, and the Lord said, "Make a fiery serpent, and set it on a pole; and it shall be that everyone who is bitten, when he looks at it, shall live."

Moses made a snake out of bronze and placed it on a pole. The sick and dying were carried from their tents so that they could see the metal snake. If they looked at the serpent, they were healed.

The bronze serpent was a representation of Jesus, the Son of God, who would someday come to this world and die to save sinful human beings from sin. When Jesus was on earth, He said, "And as Moses lifted up the serpent in the wilderness, even so must the Son of Man be lifted up, that whoever believes in Him should not perish but have eternal life" (John 3:14, 15).

At last the day came when the cavalcade made camp near the Jordan River. The people could look across the stream and see the land that had long ago been promised to the bold pioneers, Abraham, Isaac, and Jacob. At this time Moses counted the people, but in the whole camp there was not one man left of the older generation who had refused to go into the land thirty-eight years earlier. Except, that is, Caleb, the son of Jephunneh and Joshua, the son of Nun.

Moses, the aged leader, called the people together, and spoke to them of God's goodness in rescuing them from Egypt and in caring for them during the long years of wandering in the desert. He reminded them of how their fathers had died because of disobedience. He warned them that if they forgot God again and worshiped idols, they would be scattered among the nations. Moses repeated the Ten Commandments to the people so all could hear. Then he wrote them on a scroll of parchment. He also wrote down all the rules concerning the sacrifices, the clean and unclean animals, different kinds of relationships between people, and the laws of quarantine and sanitation.

Moses gave this book to the priests to keep in a safe place in the side of the golden ark. He told them that once every seven

GOD SAYS:

"Therefore the people came to Moses, and said, 'We have sinned, for we have spoken against the Lord and against you; pray to the Lord that He take away the serpents from us.' So Moses prayed for the people." –Numbers 21:7

years they were to read the laws to the people so that all might hear God's word for themselves and not depend upon the hearing of others. In those days there were no printed books, and many of the people could not read the scrolls written by scribes.

THE MAN WHO COULDN'T CURSE ISRAEL

Numbers 22–24

A s the Israelites marched into the Jordan River valley, they gained victories over the tribes who tried to stop them. They defeated their enemies and conquered many walled cities. Balak, king of Moab, heard of the triumphal march of Israel, and he was afraid. He called his chieftains to a special council.

"Now this company will lick up all that is around us, as an ox licks up the grass of the field," King Balak said to his counselors. What could he do? He decided to send for a prophet named Balaam. He would give this man a large amount of money to come and place a curse on the conquering nation of Israel.

Some of the elders of Moab and Midian went to visit Balaam with gold from the king, to flatter him and entice him to accept the king's invitation. The prophet listened to their story and then asked the men to stay the night so he could find out what he should do. He did not really need the time, because he knew that he should not go. He hoped that God would permit him to receive honor and treasure from King Balak anyway. But the Lord came to Balaam and said, "You shall not go with them; you shall not curse the people, for they are blessed."

The next morning, Balaam got up and said to the messengers, "Go back to your land; for the Lord has refused to give me permission to go with you." The prophet's words revealed that he really wanted to go with them, because he placed the blame on God for not fulfilling the king's request.

When Balak heard about the prophet's refusal, he sent men of higher rank to Balaam, urging him to accept the king's commission. When Balaam heard the second request, he said, "Though Balak were to give me his house full of silver and gold, I could not go beyond the word of the Lord my God, to do less or more. Now therefore, please, you also stay here tonight, that I may know what more the Lord will say to me." The prophet was still anxious to go, in spite of the divine

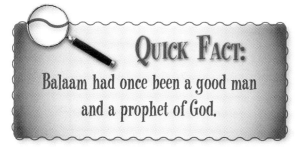

QUICK FACT:
Balaam had once been a good man and a prophet of God.

command against it. God looked into Balaam's selfish heart and told the prophet, "If the men come to call you, rise and go with them; but only the word which I speak to you—that you shall do."

In the morning Balaam was so eager to go with the princes of Moab that he didn't wait for them to ask him again. Instead, he harnessed his donkey and, with two servants, hurried away with them.

God was angry with Balaam for going with the men of Moab without them asking Him. The Lord stationed an angel on the road to stop the prophet from doing wrong.

Balaam's donkey saw the heavenly being standing in the road with a drawn sword in his hand, and she turned away into a field. Balaam hit the poor animal and turned her back to the highway.

Again the angel stood in the way, and the donkey swerved aside and crushed Balaam's foot against a stone wall. The prophet was angry, and he hit the animal again. Then the angel stood in a narrow place where the beast of burden could not turn away. When the donkey saw the angel, she lay down under Balaam. The prophet was beside himself with anger and beat the poor animal with his wooden staff. The Lord then allowed the donkey to speak, and she said to Balaam, "What have I done to you, that you have struck me these three times?"

"Because you have abused me," Balaam replied, completely outraged. "I wish there were a sword in my hand, for now I would kill you!"

The donkey said to Balaam, "Am I not your donkey on which you have ridden, ever since I became yours, to this day? Was I ever disposed to do this to you?"

"No," he said.

Then God opened Balaam's eyes, and he saw the angel standing in the road with the drawn sword in his hand. Then he humbly bowed his head and fell flat on his face.

"Why have you struck your donkey these three times?" the angel asked him. "Behold, I have come out to stand against you, because your way is perverse before Me."

"I have sinned," said Balaam, "for I did not know You stood in the way against me. Now therefore, if it displeases You, I will turn back."

Surely Balaam knew that his actions were displeasing to God, but even now he hoped he could go with the men from Moab.

THOUGHT QUESTION:
Why did the angel appear to Balaam?

The angel told Balaam, "Go with the men, but only the word that I speak to you, that you shall speak."

So, Balaam rode on to Moab, and King Balak came out to meet the prophet and honor him. The next day Balak took him to a high place on a hill overlooking the camp of

Israel. Balaam asked the king to have seven altars built, and he offered sacrifices to God. Then the prophet said he would climb up higher on the hill by himself to hear what God might tell him. He said, "Perhaps the Lord will come to meet me, and whatever He shows me I will tell you."

When Balaam returned to the king and his counselors, he began to speak. Imagine how astonished the king was when he heard the words. Balaam was not cursing Israel. He was saying,

> "How shall I curse whom God has not cursed?
> And how shall I denounce whom the Lord has
>   not denounced?
> For from the top of the rocks I see him,
> And from the hills I behold him;
> There! A people dwelling alone,
> Not reckoning itself among the nations."

The king was furious. "What have you done to me?" he asked.

"Must I not take heed to speak what the Lord has put in my mouth?" answered Balaam.

The king decided to try again, so he took Balaam to another mountain called Pisgah. Again Balak had seven altars built, and sacrifices were offered on them; but once more when Balaam spoke, he blessed Israel.

Balak took Balaam to a third place, the mountain called Peor that overlooks the desert plain. For a third time, altars were built and sacrifices offered. By this time Balaam knew that he could not curse Israel. He looked toward the Israelite camp spread out in a perfect pattern of tents, arranged by the twelve tribes. He saw the tent of meeting with the pillar of cloud above it, and again he blessed the nation. He also prophesied that the promised Savior would come as a brilliant star in the heavens. Balaam spoke these beautiful words concerning Jesus, the Savior of the human race:

> "I see Him, but not now;
> I behold Him, but not near;
> A Star shall come out of Jacob;
> A Scepter shall rise out of Israel,
> And batter the brow of Moab,
> And destroy all the sons of tumult."

Balak, the king of Moab, was very angry at Balaam, and he struck his fists together. "I called you to curse my enemies," said the king, "and look, you have bountifully blessed them these three times! Now therefore, flee to your place. I said I would greatly honor you, but in fact, the Lord has kept you back from honor."

Balaam went home without silver or gold. In spite of his attempt to curse the nation of Israel, this disobedient prophet had actually given a hopeful prophecy about the glorious future of Israel.

GOD SAYS:
" 'Did I not tell you, saying, "All that the Lord speaks, that I must do"?' "
−Numbers 23:26

THE DEATH OF MOSES

Deuteronomy 31–34

Moses was about to turn 120 years old. His brother Aaron was in his grave, and all the older generation had died except Caleb and Joshua, the two spies who had given a positive report from Canaan. Those who were small children when the spies returned from Canaan were now more than forty years old.

On Moses' 120th birthday, the Lord said to him, "Behold, the days approach when you must die; call Joshua, and present yourselves in the tabernacle of meeting, that I may inaugurate him."

Moses and Joshua stood at the entrance of the tent of meeting before all the people. Then the Lord appeared in a column of cloud that came to stand at the doorway of the tent. There the Lord gave Joshua his commission and said, "Be strong and of good courage; for you shall bring the children of Israel into the land of which I swore to them, and I will be with you."

Moses turned toward the multitude of people and announced that he must soon go to his rest. Then he recited

a beautiful poem God had given him, in the hearing of all
Israel. He told how the people had been delivered:

"Give ear, O heavens, and I will speak;
And hear, O earth, the words of my mouth.
Let my teaching drop as the rain,
My speech distill as the dew,
As raindrops on the tender herb,
And as showers on the grass.
For I proclaim the name of the Lord:
Ascribe greatness to our God.
He is the Rock, His work is perfect;
For all His ways are justice,
A God of truth and without injustice;
Righteous and upright is He.

"They have corrupted themselves;
They are not His children,
Because of their blemish:
A perverse and crooked generation.
Do you thus deal with the Lord,
O foolish and unwise people?
Is He not your Father, who bought you?
Has He not made you and established you?

"Remember the days of old,
Consider the years of many generations.
Ask your father, and he will show you;
Your elders, and they will tell you:
When the Most High divided their inheritance
    to the nations,
When He separated the sons of Adam,
He set the boundaries of the peoples
According to the number of the children of
    Israel.
For the Lord's portion is His people;
Jacob is the place of His inheritance.

"He found him in a desert land
And in the wasteland, a howling wilderness;
He encircled him, He instructed him,
He kept him as the apple of His eye.
As an eagle stirs up its nest,
Hovers over its young,
Spreading out its wings, taking them up,
Carrying them on its wings,
So the Lord alone led him,
And there was no foreign god with him.

"He made him ride in the heights of the earth,
That he might eat the produce of the fields;
He made him draw honey from the rock,
And oil from the flinty rock."

When Moses had finished reciting his beautiful ode, he again spoke to the people, instructing them as if they were his own children. He told them, "Set your hearts on all the words which I testify among you today, which you shall command your children to be careful to observe—all the words of this law. For it is not a futile thing for you, because it is your life."

God called on Moses to climb the mountain that very day. He walked alone out of the camp and started up the trail leading to the summit of Mount Nebo. Thousands of men, women, and children stood watching with teary eyes as the solitary figure grew smaller in the distance. They had grumbled and complained so many times against this great man. So many times he had prayed for God to spare their lives! Now he was leaving his people, and they would go into their homeland without him.

From the top of the mountain, Moses looked with undimmed eyes into the land of Canaan. He saw the green valleys

GOD SAYS:

" 'Be strong and of good courage, for you must go with this people to the land which the Lord has sworn to their fathers to give them.' "
—Deuteronomy 31:7

and meadows, the rolling hills and forests. Far to the north loomed snow-covered Mount Hermon. He could see the

THOUGHT QUESTION:

Why did God raise Moses from the dead and take him to heaven?

river Jordan, the Dead Sea, and the rugged mountains to the east.

After the aged prophet had seen all this, he was content to go to his rest. The Bible gives this record, "Moses the servant of the Lord died there in the land of Moab, according to the word of the Lord. And He buried him in a valley in the land of Moab, opposite Beth Peor; but no one knows his grave to this day."

If Moses had remained in Egypt, he might have had a spectacular royal funeral when he died, and his body would have been embalmed and placed in one of the rooms in a pyramid. But Moses chose to endure hardships and suffering with his people. He loved God more than riches and the honor of human beings.

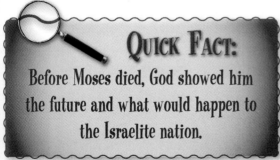

QUICK FACT:

Before Moses died, God showed him the future and what would happen to the Israelite nation.

He did not long remain in the grave, because God raised him to life and took him to heaven. The Bible tells us in Luke 9 that when Jesus was on earth, Moses and Elijah came from heaven and stood by the Son of God when He was transfigured. Moses lives today in the eternal paradise of God.

RAHAB PROTECTS THE SPIES

Joshua 1; 2

A fter Israel had mourned the death of Moses for thirty days, Joshua, the new leader, commanded the people to get ready to enter Canaan. Officers went through the camp giving the people this instruction: "Prepare provisions for yourselves, for within three days you will cross over this Jordan, to go in to possess the land which the Lord your God is giving you to possess."

Joshua knew that he must take the frontier cities on the other side of the Jordan River before he could conquer the enemies that lived in the interior of the country. He sent two men to Jericho, the first city, to study the situation. They entered the city gate and walked along the narrow streets, feeling strange among the foreign people. Soon they found that they were being watched. Curious men began to follow them to see where they were going. The Israelite men quickened their pace, but so did the men who followed them. Someone hurried away to tell the king that spies from the camp of Israel were in the town. While out of sight for a few moments, the spies turned in at an open doorway and met a woman named Rahab. She welcomed them when they told her that they were Israelites.

"I know that the Lord has given you the land," she said to the spies, "that the terror of you has fallen on us, and that all the inhabitants of the land are fainthearted because of you. For we have heard how the Lord dried up the water of the Red Sea for you when you came out of Egypt, and what you did to the two kings of the Amorites who were on the other side of the Jordan, Sihon and Og, whom you utterly destroyed. And as soon as we heard these things, our hearts melted; neither did there remain any more courage in anyone because of you, for the Lord your God, He is God in heaven above and on earth beneath."

> ## GOD SAYS:
> " 'Be strong and of good courage; do not be afraid, nor be dismayed, for the Lord your God is with you wherever you go.' " –Joshua 1:9

Soon officers from the king of Jericho arrived at Rahab's house and said to her, "Bring out the men who have come to you, who have entered your house, for they have come to search out all the country."

Rahab admitted that the spies had been in her house, but she told the officers to hurry on and pursue them into the country. Actually, she had hidden the two men under piles of flax that were drying on the flat roof of her house. When the officers had gone, she called the men down from their hiding place and said to them, "Now therefore, I beg you, swear to me by the Lord, since I have shown you kindness, that you also will show kindness to my father's house, and give me a true token, and spare my father, my mother, my brothers, my sisters, and all that they have, and deliver our lives from death."

The men replied to her, "Our lives for yours, if none of you tell this business of ours. And it shall be, when the Lord has given us the land, that we will deal kindly and truly with you."

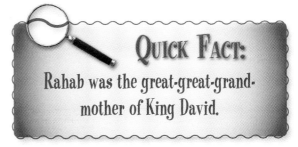

QUICK FACT:
Rahab was the great-great-grandmother of King David.

Because of her kindness in sparing their lives, the men gave Rahab this promise: "When we come into the land, you bind this line of scarlet cord in the window through which you let us down, and . . . bring your father, your mother, your brothers, and all your father's household to your own home. So it shall be that whoever goes outside the doors of your house into the street, his blood shall be on his own head, and we will be guiltless. And whoever is with you in the house, his blood shall be on our head if a hand is laid on him. And if you tell this business of ours, then we will be free from your oath which you made us swear."

Rahab's house was built on the wide city wall. When it was dark, she let the two spies down to the ground outside the city by a rope from her window. At Rahab's suggestion, the spies hurried off to the nearby hills and remained in hiding for three days until the officers of the city were no longer searching for them. Then they returned to the camp of Israel and gave their report. "Truly the Lord has delivered all the land into our hands," they said to Joshua, "for indeed all the inhabitants of the country are faint-hearted because of us."

Joshua knew that the Israelite nation faced a great test. Would the people have courage when they advanced against the enemy, or would they lose heart as their fathers had done thirty-eight years before? That night Joshua prayed for strength to be a good leader. The words God had spoken to him came back to his mind. "Have I not commanded you? Be strong and of good courage; do not be afraid, nor be dismayed, for the Lord your God is with you wherever you go."

CROSSING THE JORDAN RIVER

Joshua 3–6:7

The next morning the people marched forward to the banks of the Jordan River not far from the city of Jericho. After they had camped for three days, the leaders went to each tribe and told the people to be ready to advance when they saw the priests take up the golden ark.

At a signal from Joshua, the priests marched ahead with the ark, and the people followed in an orderly procession behind them. The river had no bridges or ferryboats for crossing, and at that time of year it was flooded from bank to bank. Crossing the river looked impossible. But when the feet of the priests touched the muddy waters of the river, the water plunging toward them from upstream came to a stop and formed a wall. The water that had already rushed by flowed on downstream, leaving dry ground so that the people could cross over in safety.

The priests carrying the ark walked to the middle of the dry bed in the river Jordan and stopped. They waited until the huge multitude of people with their herds of cows and flocks of other animals had marched by them and reached the other side. Then the Lord told Joshua to choose twelve men, one from each tribe, for a special task. Joshua summoned twelve men and said to them, "Cross over before the ark of the Lord your God into the midst of the Jordan, and each one of you take up a stone on his shoulder, according to the number of the tribes of the children of Israel."

The twelve men took the stones from the bed of the river and carried them up the riverbank. They piled them up as a monument at Gilgal, where Israel camped that night. Joshua told the people, "When your children ask their fathers in time to come, saying, 'What are these stones?' then you shall let your children know, saying, 'Israel crossed over this Jordan on dry land, . . . that all the peoples of the earth may know the hand of the Lord, that it is mighty, that you may fear the Lord your God forever.' "

> ## GOD SAYS:
>
> "And Joshua said to the people, 'Sanctify yourselves, for tomorrow the Lord will do wonders among you.' "
> —Joshua 3:5

The Israelites had entered the Promised Land. Feeling very thankful, they spent seven days celebrating the Passover Feast, which reminded them of their deliverance from Egypt. The people were able to get grain that was grown in that country, so the manna stopped. For forty years the food from heaven had appeared every day of the week except the seventh day, the Sabbath. From this day on, the Israelites would live on the produce of Canaan.

Joshua walked outside the camp to study how his army might capture the city of Jericho. The city was closed tightly in case of an attack from the Israelites. Suddenly he saw a man standing opposite him with a drawn sword in his hand. Joshua approached the warrior and said, "Are You for us or for our adversaries?"

"No," He said, "but as Commander of the army of the Lord I have now come."

Joshua knelt on the ground and bowed his head, saying, "What does my Lord say to His servant?"

"Take your sandal off your foot," the Commander of the Lord's army said to Joshua, "for the place where you stand is holy." Joshua removed his sandals.

God gave these instructions to Joshua: "See! I have given Jericho into your hand, its king, and the mighty men of valor. You shall march around the city, all you men of war; you shall go all around the city once." They were to go on this march once a day for six days, with priests carrying the ark and seven priests each holding a ram's horn. On the seventh day the army would march around the city seven times, while the seven priests blew the horns. After the seventh time, the priests would blow a long blast on the horns, and when the people heard it, all of them at once would raise a mighty shout. At that moment the wall of the city would fall down so that the Israelites could march right in.

When Joshua heard this instruction, he was very happy. Now he knew God's plan for taking the walled city. He called the priests to him and commanded them to prepare to carry the golden ark and also to appoint seven priests who would carry rams' horns. They were to start marching around the city of Jericho immediately.

THOUGHT QUESTION:
How can we remember the things God has done for us?

CONQUEST OF JERICHO

Joshua 6:8–7:1

In the city of Jericho, a fever of excitement was building up. "Have you heard the bad news?" a man asked his neighbor. "The Israelites are coming. Although the river is flooded, the whole nation of Israel crossed over it. The river actually stopped flowing, and the people marched across the dry riverbed!"

The citizens of Jericho were afraid that they would soon be attacked. The gates of the city were closed and barred. No one was allowed to enter, and no one could leave.

In the house of Rahab, which was built in the wall of Jericho, there was excitement, as well. Every morning Rahab went to the window facing the countryside to see that the scarlet rope was in plain sight. Looking out of a window that opened above the city wall, she could see the soldiers of Jericho with their swords and spears, guarding the wall.

One morning Rahab heard rams' horns sounding in the distance. Soon a strange procession appeared. A column of Israelite soldiers was leading the procession, and priests dressed in white came marching behind, carrying a chest covered by a big cloth. In the morning sunlight the

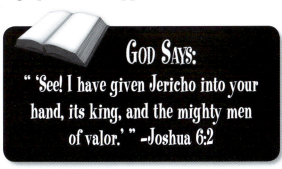

GOD SAYS:
" 'See! I have given Jericho into your hand, its king, and the mighty men of valor.' " –Joshua 6:2

soldiers' armor shone in rich splendor. Behind the ark came more soldiers in full battle gear.

Feeling both happiness and anxiety, Rahab watched the approaching cavalcade. She could not hear any sounds from the soldiers or the priests carrying the ark, because seven priests were blowing their rams' horns, and the sound echoed through the valley. Around the walled city, the men of Israel marched. After they had circled the city, all was quiet. The procession disappeared in

the direction of the Israelite camp. Rahab wondered what might happen next. Would the soldiers attack the city? Would Rahab and her family be spared, as the spies had promised?

The next morning the soldiers and priests came marching again. Every morning for six days, Rahab saw the same column of men go marching by. The soldiers of Jericho, looking down from the wall, began to make jokes about the men of Israel. They must have said that the Israelites were afraid to fight.

During the week, Rahab had gathered her relatives into her house. On the seventh morning Rahab and her family watched the soldiers marching by, and the priests carrying the ark moving with determined steps. On this day, however, the procession did not stop when it had gone around the city once. It kept on marching, marching, marching, until it had circled the wall of Jericho seven times. Then the priests blew their horns, and the vast throng of Israel, who had been gathered nearby, gave a mighty shout. The shout echoed through the valley and mingled with a terrible rumbling sound. When the shout died away, the rumbling grew louder and louder. The walls of Jericho shook and then crumbled and fell with a thunderous roar! The soldiers of Israel ran forward and quickly overtook the city, killing all the inhabitants and taking the silver and gold for the treasury of the Lord. Every building was burned except the house of Rahab.

THOUGHT QUESTION: Why were Rahab and her family not harmed when Jericho was captured?

Joshua gave this command to the spies: "Bring out the woman and all that she has, as you swore to her."

When the two spies arrived at the house in the city wall, they found Rahab and all the members of her family waiting for the promised protectors to arrive. Rahab's family was welcomed in the camp of Israel, because the people had heard how she saved the lives of the spies. Rahab believed in God, and later she married a man of Israel named Salmon. She became the great-great-grandmother of David, king of Israel.

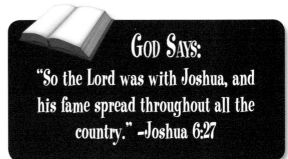

GOD SAYS:
"So the Lord was with Joshua, and his fame spread throughout all the country." –Joshua 6:27

Joshua had given strict orders to all the people that no one should take any loot from the city of Jericho. Through the power of God the enemy had been conquered. Therefore, the people did not deserve any of the treasure for themselves.

Before Moses died he had told the people, "Be sure your sin will find you out" (Numbers 32:23). No one can hide from the eyes of God. But there was a man of the tribe of Judah named Achan who had forgotten these words. He went into the city to destroy the enemy; as he made his way among the smoking ruins, he saw a bag of silver and gold spilled in the street. He looked at the treasure and was filled with greed. There was no one watching, he thought, so he knelt down and began putting the gold and silver into the bag. He also found a beautiful robe and hid it under his coat. Then he ran as fast as he could toward the camp of Israel.

A TRAITOR IN THE CAMP

Joshua 7:2–8:30

Another city called Ai (ay-eye), smaller than Jericho, lay ahead. Joshua said to a few of his men, "Go up and spy out the country." The warriors stealthily surveyed the town and returned to their leader, saying, "Do not let all the people go up, but let about two or three thousand men go up and attack Ai. Do not weary all the people [of Israel] there, for the people of Ai are few."

So, about three thousand soldiers marched up to take the city; but the men of Ai came out and fought savagely, killing thirty-six Israelite soldiers before the army fled in defeat. When the soldiers of Israel heard about the disaster that had befallen their comrades, their courage disappeared. Joshua mourned and fell on his face before the sacred ark, calling on the Lord for help.

God said to Joshua, "Get up! Why do you lie thus on your face? Israel has sinned, and they have also transgressed My covenant which I commanded them. For they have even taken some of the accursed things, and have both stolen and deceived; and they have also put it among their own stuff. Therefore the children of Israel could not stand before their enemies, but turned their backs before their enemies. . . . Neither will I be with you anymore, unless you destroy the accursed from among you."

When Joshua found out that someone had stolen treasure from Jericho, he called all the people of Israel together and had them gather by tribe. God had instructed

him to use a method called casting lots, which is similar to drawing straws, to find the guilty person. As the leaders cast lots, the results showed that the culprit was a member of the tribe of Judah. They continued to cast lots until they had narrowed down the field of suspects to the man named Achan. He was

THOUGHT QUESTION:

Can we hide anything from God?

the traitor in the camp. Joshua said to Achan, "My son, I beg you, give glory to the Lord God of Israel, and make confession to Him, and tell me now what you have done; do not hide it from me."

Achan confessed to Joshua, "Indeed I have sinned against the Lord God of Israel, and this is what I have done: When I saw among the spoils a beautiful Babylonian garment, two hundred shekels of silver, and a wedge of gold weighing fifty shekels, I coveted them and took them. And there they are, hidden in the earth in the midst of my tent, with the silver under it."

Joshua sent some men to Achan's tent, and they found the money and the piece of clothing in a hole in the ground. Then Achan and his family and all he possessed were taken outside the camp to the Valley of Achor, and Joshua said, "Why have you troubled us? The Lord will trouble you this day."

Achan had disobeyed instructions in a time of war, and he had broken the law of the Lord. The traitor was stoned to death by the men of Israel.

Then the Lord said to Joshua, "Do not be afraid, nor be dismayed; take all the people of war with you, and arise, go up to Ai. See, I have given into your hand the king of Ai, his people, his city, and his land. And you shall do to Ai and its king as you did to Jericho and its king. Only its spoil and its cattle you shall take as booty for yourselves. Lay an ambush for the city behind it."

Joshua, the mighty warrior, instructed the leaders of thirty thousand fighting men to hide near Ai and sent them out at night. The next morning Joshua took command of about five thousand men, and they marched up to the gate of Ai. When the king of the city saw the small army with Joshua, he hurried out through the city gate with every man from the city of Ai and attacked the Israelites. Joshua's men turned and ran toward the desert, pretending they were beaten. A fierce battle cry echoed through the valley as the soldiers of Ai rushed in pursuit of the retreating men. They were so sure of victory that they left the city open and undefended.

Then, as God had instructed him, Joshua lifted his javelin high and pointed it toward Ai. That was the signal for the thirty thousand soldiers who were in hiding to come out and take the city. They marched through the open gates, conquered the city, and burned it. At that moment the fleeing army of Israel turned on the soldiers of Ai; and when the enemy saw their city

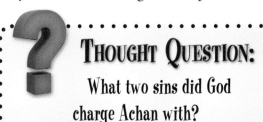

THOUGHT QUESTION:
What two sins did God charge Achan with?

going up in flames, they lost heart and gave up. The Israelites killed all the people of the town, as God had told them to, and left the dead king of Ai on a pile of stones at the entrance to the destroyed city.

WHEN THE SUN STOOD STILL

Joshua 9–10:15

Fear came over all the kings in the highlands and lowlands of Canaan when they heard how the conquering heroes of Israel had defeated their enemies. The Lord went before His people, as He had promised, and they won victory after victory.

When the inhabitants of Gibeon heard what Joshua had done to Jericho and Ai, they decided on a plan to save their lives. Although their city was less than twenty miles from the camp of Israel, some men from Gibeon disguised themselves by wearing old clothes and worn-out sandals and went to the camp. They loaded their pack animals with old sacks and patched wineskins. They put dry and moldy bread in their saddlebags. Then they set out on the short journey to Gilgal, where they met Joshua. They made themselves known by saying, "We have come from a far country; now therefore, make a covenant with us."

The leaders of Israel, thinking that these ambassadors might be telling a lie, said, "Perhaps you dwell among us; so how can we make a covenant with you?"

"We are your servants," they said to Joshua.

So Joshua asked them, "Who are you, and where do you come from?"

QUICK FACT:
God had told the Israelites not to make any kind of agreement with the nations of Canaan.

Then the Gibeonites deceived the leaders of Israel, saying, "From a very far country your servants have come, because of the name of the Lord your God; for we have heard of His fame, and all that He did in Egypt, and all that He did to the two kings of the Amorites who were beyond the Jordan—to Sihon king of Heshbon, and Og king of Bashan, who was at Ashtaroth. Therefore our elders and all

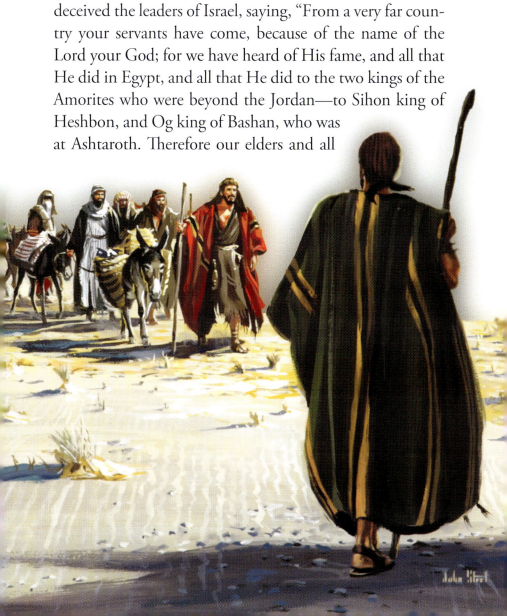

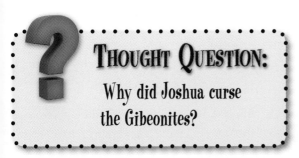

the inhabitants of our country spoke to us, saying, 'Take provisions with you for the journey, and go to meet them, and say to them, "We are your servants; now therefore, make a covenant with us." ' This bread of ours we took hot for our provision from our houses on the day we departed to come to you. But now look, it is dry and moldy. And these wineskins which we filled were new, and see, they are torn; and these our garments and our sandals have become old because of the very long journey."

When the leaders of Israel saw this evidence of a long journey, they accepted the story and made peace terms with the foreigners without seeking advice from the Lord. But three days later, Joshua and his officers learned the truth—the people were Canaanites who actually lived only a few miles away. When the people of Israel heard how the leaders had been deceived, they complained about it. But Joshua declared that a promise made must be kept.

He summoned the leaders of Gibeon and said to them, "Why have you deceived us, saying, 'We are very far from you,' when you dwell near us? Now therefore, you are cursed, and none of you shall be freed from being slaves—woodcutters and water carriers for the house of my God."

They answered Joshua, "Because it was certainly told your servants that the Lord your God commanded His servant Moses to give you all the land, and to destroy all the inhabitants of the land from before you; therefore we were very much afraid for our lives because of you, and have done this thing. And now, here we are, in your hands; do with us as it seems good and right to do to us." From that day the Gibeonites became servants in the camp of Israel.

Not long afterward, the kings of five other cities in Canaan assembled their armies and marched against the people of Gibeon, because that city had made a peace treaty with Israel. The Gibeonites sent a message to Joshua at Gilgal, saying, "Do not forsake your servants; come up to us quickly, save us and help us, for all the kings of the Amorites who dwell in the mountains have gathered together against us."

God told Joshua that he should go to Gibeon and that the Canaanite armies would be defeated. Quickly mustering his army, Joshua marched all night and made a surprise attack on the enemy. The army of Israel threw the enemy into a panic, and they fled. A hailstorm, prepared by the Lord, killed many of the defeated soldiers. More of them died from the hailstones than from the swords of the Israelites.

All day long the army of Israel chased the Canaanites along the road, and Joshua pleaded for more time to finish the battle. The Bible says, "The sun stood still in the midst of heaven, and did not hasten to go down for about a whole day. And there has been no day like that, before it

GOD SAYS:
" 'So the sun stood still, and the moon stopped, till the people had revenge upon their enemies.' " –Joshua 10:13

or after it, that the Lord heeded the voice of a man; for the Lord fought for Israel." The conquering army thanked God for victory over their enemies, and Joshua led his warriors back to their camp in Gilgal.

DIVIDING THE CONQUERED LAND

Joshua 10:29–24:33

Joshua led the nation of Israel to other cities in Canaan. The army defeated thirty-one kings who held territory from the desert south of Beersheba to the northern highlands near Mount Hermon. Then "the land rested from war."

Not all the enemies had been conquered, but the time had come for the Promised Land to be divided among the twelve tribes. Each tribe would vanquish the enemies that remained in its own territory.

The assignments of land were drawn by each tribe, according to lot. When the tribe of Judah came for its inheritance, Caleb, the faithful spy who had stood with Joshua to give a good report of the land, made this request: "And now, behold, the Lord has kept me alive, as He said, these forty-five years, ever since the Lord spoke this word to Moses while Israel wandered in the wilderness; and now, here I am this day, eighty-five years old. As yet I am as strong this day as I was on the day that Moses sent me; just as my strength was then, so now is my strength for war, both for going out and for coming in. Now therefore, give me this mountain of which the Lord spoke in that day; for you heard in that day how the Anakim were there, and that the cities were great and fortified. It may be that the Lord will be with me, and I shall be able to drive them out as the Lord said."

Caleb was asking for the walled cities of the giants! Although he was eighty-five years old, he knew that God would help him conquer these fierce people.

Caleb had a beautiful daughter named Achsah. He said to the valiant young warriors, "Whoever attacks Kirjath Sepher and takes it, to him I will give Achsah my daughter as wife."

Now Othniel, a brave young man, loved Achsah. Taking a band of men with him, he captured this city of the giants, and Othniel received Caleb's daughter to be his wife.

When each tribe had received its share of the land, Joshua asked for one city that was still unassigned. It was Timnath Serah, which means, "That which is left."

Years of peace came to the nation of Israel. The people gathered in Shiloh and set up the tent of meeting, and they offered sacrifices and worshiped the Lord.

A day came when Joshua, who was advanced in age by now, realized that his leadership was nearing an end, so he summoned the head men of the tribes and said to them,

Thought Question:
Why didn't the Levites receive a share of the land?

"I am old, advanced in age. You have seen all that the Lord your God has done to all these nations because of you, for the Lord your God is He who has fought for you. See, I have divided to you by lot these nations that remain, to be an inheritance for your tribes, from the Jordan, with all the nations that I have cut off, as far as the Great Sea westward. And the Lord your God will expel them from before you and drive them out of your sight. So you shall possess their land, as the Lord your God promised you. Therefore be very courageous to keep and to do all that is written in the Book of the Law of Moses, lest you turn aside from it to the right hand or to the left, and lest you go among these nations, these who remain among you. You shall not make mention of the name of their gods, nor cause anyone to swear by them; you shall not serve them nor bow down to them, but you shall hold fast to the Lord your God, as you have done to this day."

Joshua added this testimony concerning the Lord's care for the nation: "Behold, this day I am going the way of all the earth. And you know in all your hearts and in all your souls that not one thing has failed of all the good things which

QUICK FACT:

Caleb was the oldest man in Israel, yet he was the only one who had the courage to take on the giants.

the Lord your God spoke concerning you. All have come to pass for you, and not one word of them has failed."

Then Joshua called for all the people to assemble at Shechem. He told them how Abraham had made his first home at Shechem when he entered the land of promise. He reminded them of God's care and protection to their

fathers during the long years in Egypt, how He had delivered them and cared for them through the wandering in the desert. He gave thanks to the Lord for the victory they had won over their ene-

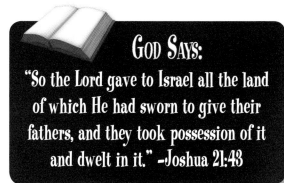

GOD SAYS:

"So the Lord gave to Israel all the land of which He had sworn to give their fathers, and they took possession of it and dwelt in it." –Joshua 21:43

mies. To the throng of people he said, "Choose for yourselves this day whom you will serve. . . . But as for me and my house, we will serve the Lord."

The people shouted, "We also will serve the Lord, for He is our God."

Joshua wrote the pledge of Israel in the book of the Law that was kept in the side of the ark. Then he set up a great stone as a monument and said, "Behold, this stone shall be a witness to us, for it has heard all the words of the Lord which He spoke to us. It shall therefore be a witness to you, lest you deny your God."

Joshua died at the age of 110 years. He was buried with great honor in the city of Timnath Serah, which had been given to him as his possession.

About this time, the bones of Joseph, which had been brought from Egypt, were buried in Shechem, the city given to the descendants of Joseph as their inheritance. Joseph's final resting place was a plot of land bought by his father Jacob from Hamor, the son of the city's founder, Shechem, centuries earlier.

A WOMAN SAVES THE NATION

Judges 4; 5

When Joshua died, there was no strong leader in Israel to take his place. Soon the men who had worked with him passed to their rest. Then Israel forgot God and refused to obey the Ten Commandments. The people began to worship idols as the Canaanites did. They bowed before the god Baal and the goddess Ashtoreth.

The tribes were settled in their own land, but now they were separated from one another more than they had ever been before. They lost their unity and their strength as a nation. It was possible for enemies to attack the different tribes, steal their crops, and leave whole communities in terror.

In order to save Israel, God called some individuals to champion the truth and to deliver the people from their enemies. These leaders were known as judges. The land usually enjoyed peace and security during the rule of the judges; but there were periods when there was no judge, and in those times the people forgot God and practiced idolatry.

One of the most famous judges who conquered the enemies of Israel was a woman named Deborah. She was a prophet as well as a judge, and her husband's name was Lapidoth. Sitting under a palm tree between Ramah and Bethel, she would listen to the cases brought to her by the people of Israel. She was a wise and influential woman who trusted in the Lord.

A powerful enemy, Jabin, king of Canaan, had oppressed the people of Israel for twenty years with his army of nine hundred iron chariots and thousands of soldiers. His attacks against Israel were led by a general named Sisera. One day Deborah sent for Barak, a leader and Israelite soldier. She asked him, "Has not the Lord God of Israel commanded, saying, 'Go and deploy troops at Mount Tabor; take with you ten thousand men. . . . Against you I will deploy Sisera, the commander of Jabin's army, with his chariots and his multitude at the River Kishon; and I will deliver him into your hand'?"

Showing almost no courage, Barak replied, "If you will go with me, then I will go; but if you will not go with me, I will not go."

"I will surely go with you," Deborah replied. "Nevertheless there will be no glory for you in the journey you are taking, for the Lord will sell Sisera into the hand of a woman."

So, Deborah and Barak led the Israelite army toward Mount Tabor. When Sisera heard that the warriors of Israel were on the march, he came out with his nine hundred chariots to meet them. Deborah saw the evil hordes approaching and said to Barak, "Up! For this is the day in which the Lord has delivered Sisera into your hand. Has not the Lord gone out before you?"

Leading his ten thousand men in a fierce charge, Barak rushed down the mountainside to attack the enemy. Men on horses clashed with men on the ground. The soldiers in iron chariots dashed into the fight. But the Canaanites soon saw that they were being defeated. Sisera, the enemy general, jumped from his chariot and ran for his life. Barak and his army chased after the beaten soldiers and caught up with them at the town of Harosheth Hagoyim; all of them were killed. But in the confusion they did not see Sisera escape.

The defeated general ran northward and found refuge in the tent of Heber, a Kenite tribesman. Now Heber was away, but Jael, his wife, met the weary general at the tent entrance. She said to him, "Turn aside, my lord, turn aside to me; do not fear."

The general stepped into the tent and sat down, because he was tired and thirsty. The woman wrapped a blanket around him.

"Please give me a little water to drink," he said to her.

Instead of giving Sisera some water, Jael opened a jug of milk and gave him that to drink. Then the tired general wanted to lie down and sleep. "Stand at the door of the tent," he instructed her, "and if any man comes and inquires of you, and says, 'Is there any man here?' you shall say, 'No.' "

As soon as Sisera fell asleep, Jael picked up a big tent peg, and taking a hammer in her other hand, she stole up softly to the general and pounded the great pin through the temples of his head, so that it went into the ground beneath him.

QUICK FACT:
When Israel repented and called on the Lord, He sent leaders or judges to free them and help them remain true to God.

If Jael had given Sisera a drink of water, she could not have killed him as she intended. The customs of the people in that country were such that if a cup of water were given to a visitor, he was safe as long as he was in the tent as a guest. So, she had given him milk instead.

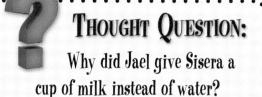

THOUGHT QUESTION: Why did Jael give Sisera a cup of milk instead of water?

Soon Barak and his men came hurrying along in pursuit of the general, and Jael went out to meet them. She said, "Come, I will show you the man whom you seek."

Barak went into the tent and found Sisera dead by the hand of the woman. Soon after, Israel's great victory over King Jabin's army was celebrated throughout the land of Israel, and Deborah wrote a song commemorating the battle. In the words, she gave glory to Jael:

> "Most blessed among women is Jael,
> The wife of Heber the Kenite;
> Blessed is she among women in tents.
> He asked for water, she gave milk;
> She brought out cream in a lordly bowl.
> She stretched her hand to the tent peg,
> Her right hand to the workmen's hammer;
> She pounded Sisera, she pierced his head,
> She split and struck through his temple.
> At her feet he sank, he fell, he lay still;
> At her feet he sank, he fell;
> Where he sank, there he fell dead."

GIDEON'S CALL TO ARMS

Judges 6–7:7

After forty years of peace and prosperity, the people of Israel again began to worship idols. God permitted another enemy to attack the nation. This time the armies of the king of Midian overran the country. No one was safe in his house or in the field. Midianites were everywhere. The attacks became so bad that the Israelites fled to caves and dens and other places in the mountains, anywhere they could hide from the enemy. For seven years the invaders swarmed over the country like grasshoppers, ruining the farms and houses. In this time of trouble the people remembered the Lord and called on Him for help. He sent a prophet through the country with a message:

"Thus says the Lord God of Israel: 'I brought you up from Egypt and brought you out of the house of bondage; and I delivered you out of the hand of the Egyptians and out of the hand of all who oppressed you, and drove them out before you and gave you their land. Also I said to you, "I am the Lord your God; do not fear the gods of the

Amorites, in whose land you dwell." But you have not obeyed My voice.' "

Soon after this pronouncement, a young man of the tribe of Manasseh, who was loyal to God, was threshing some wheat in a winepress. Gideon was keeping the grain hidden from the Midianites, because if they found it, they would take it from him. While he was at work, an angel appeared and said to him, "The Lord is with you, you mighty man of valor!"

"O my lord," Gideon replied, "if the Lord is with us, why then has all this happened to us? And where are all His miracles which our fathers told us about, saying, 'Did not the Lord bring us up from Egypt?' But now the Lord has forsaken us and delivered us into the hands of the Midianites."

God Says:

"Then the children of Israel did evil in the sight of the Lord. So the Lord delivered them into the hand of Midian for seven years." -Judges 6:1

Then God Himself spoke to Gideon. "Go in this might of yours, and you shall save Israel from the hand of the Midianites. Have I not sent you?"

Trying to excuse himself, Gideon said, "O my Lord, how can I save Israel? Indeed my clan is the weakest in Manasseh, and I am the least in my father's house."

The Lord reassured him, saying, "Surely I will be with you, and you shall defeat the Midianites as one man."

Gideon wanted to be sure that he really was receiving instruction from God, so he said, "Do not depart from here, I pray, until I come to You and bring out my offering and set it before You." From his house he brought an offering of goat meat and unleavened bread. The angel of God told him to place the offering on a flat rock. Gideon set it down and poured a pot of gravy over the food. Then the angel stretched out the staff he was holding, touched the meat and bread, and fire burst out of the rock. The food was completely burned up. The angel vanished, but Gideon now knew that it was the angel of the Lord who had spoken to him.

"Alas, O Lord God!" Gideon said. "For I have seen the Angel of the Lord face to face."

But God said to him, "Peace be with you; do not fear, you shall not die."

Gideon built an altar and worshiped God in that place. Then the Lord sent him to his father's house with these instructions: "Take your father's young bull, the second bull of seven years old, and tear down the altar of Baal that your father has, and cut down the wooden image that is beside it." Gideon was to build an altar to God on the same spot and sacrifice the young bull on it. The young man did as he was told, but he waited until the middle of the night because he was afraid of his father, Joash, and the other people in his town.

In the morning the Baal worshipers in the town found their altar destroyed. They shouted angrily, "Who has done this thing?"

They asked around and discovered that it was Gideon, the son of Joash, who had destroyed the altar of Baal. The men surrounded the house of Joash and said, "Bring out your son, that he may die, because he has torn down the altar of Baal, and because he has cut down the wooden image that was beside it."

Joash, who knew that he had been doing wrong in allowing the worship of Baal, replied, "Would you plead for Baal? Would you save him? Let the one who would plead for him be put to death by morning! If he is a god, let him plead for

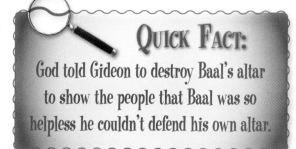

QUICK FACT:
God told Gideon to destroy Baal's altar to show the people that Baal was so helpless he couldn't defend his own altar.

himself, because his altar has been torn down!" When they heard this, none of the townspeople harmed Gideon.

Soon the Midianites and the Amalekites gathered all their fighting men together and marched toward Israel. They set up camp in the Valley of Jezreel. At that time, the Spirit of God filled young Gideon with great courage. He blew a trumpet to summon the people around him to arms. He sent messengers to the tribes of Manasseh, Asher, Zebulun, and Naphtali asking for army volunteers.

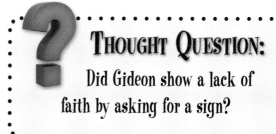

THOUGHT QUESTION: Did Gideon show a lack of faith by asking for a sign?

Gideon decided he needed more proof that God would be with him in battle. He said to the Lord, "If You will save Israel by my hand as You have said—look, I shall put a fleece of wool on the threshing floor; if there is dew on the fleece only, and it is dry on all the ground, then I shall know that You will save Israel by my hand, as You have said."

The next morning he got up early and went to find the fleece. It was so wet that he wrung out a bowlful of water from it; but the ground was dry.

Gideon still wasn't completely sure, so he said to God, "Do not be angry with me, and let me speak just once more: Let me test, I pray, just once more with the fleece; let it now be dry only on the fleece, but on all the ground let there be dew."

He hurried out of his tent the next morning and found heavy dew on the ground, but the fleece was dry. Now Gideon was sure of his mission. He knew he faced a powerful enemy, but God had promised the victory even though the Israelite army was much smaller and not as well equipped. Gideon was ready to advance by faith.

A BATTLE WITH PITCHERS AND TORCHES

Judges 7

Gideon was making plans to attack the Midianites when God gave him a strange message. The Lord said, "The people who are with you are too many for Me to give the Midianites into their hands, lest Israel claim glory for itself against Me, saying, 'My own hand has saved me.' Now therefore, proclaim in the hearing of the people, saying, 'Whoever is fearful and afraid, let him turn and depart at once from Mount Gilead.' "

Calling all his volunteer soldiers together, Gideon told them what God had said. His heart sank as he saw twenty-two thousand men pick up their swords, spears, and bags of food and start for their homes. Only ten thousand men were left to attack the hundreds of thousands of the enemy. But the Lord said to Gideon, "The people are still too many; bring them down to the water, and I will test them for you there. Then it will be, that of whom I say to you, 'This one shall go with you,' the same shall go with you; and of whomever I say to you, 'This one shall not go with you,' the same shall not go."

Gideon marched his men down to the river, and God told him to watch them drink. He should make one group of those who hurried across the stream toward the enemy camp, lapping up water as they advanced. Those who knelt by the riverbank and drank in a leisurely way, he would put in another group. Only three hundred men lapped the water with their tongues. God said to Gideon, "By the three hundred men who lapped I will save you, and deliver the Midianites into your hand. Let all the other people go, every man to his place."

The three hundred men must have wondered what was happening when they heard Gideon issue the order that another nine thousand seven hundred soldiers should return to their homes. How would he fight the Midianites with this handful of warriors?

God told Gideon that the time had come to defeat the Midianites. "But if you are afraid . . . ," the Lord said, "go down to the camp with Purah your servant, and you shall hear what they say; and afterward your hands shall be strengthened to go down against the camp."

That night Gideon and his servant went to spy on the enemy camp. The Midianites were spread out in the valley like a huge horde of locusts, and they had as many camels as the sand on the seashore. Gideon crept up to the side of one of the enemy tents, and he heard a man say to a companion, "I have had a dream: To my surprise, a loaf

GOD SAYS:
"The Lord said to Gideon, 'The people who are with you are too many for Me to give the Midianites into their hands.' " –Judges 7:2

123

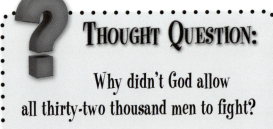

THOUGHT QUESTION:

Why didn't God allow all thirty-two thousand men to fight?

of barley bread tumbled into the camp of Midian; it came to a tent and struck it so that it fell and overturned, and the tent collapsed."

His comrade responded, "This is nothing else but the sword of Gideon the son of Joash, a man of Israel! Into his hand God has delivered Midian and the whole camp."

Gideon prayed a silent prayer of thanks to God and then slipped away and returned to his camp. As soon as he got back, he gave the command: "Arise, for the Lord has delivered the camp of Midian into your hand!"

Gideon divided his force of three hundred men into three groups. The men tried to look like soldiers ready to

fight, although the only equipment they had was an empty pitcher with a torch inside, and a trumpet.

"Look at me," Gideon said to his men, "and do likewise; watch, and when I come to the edge of the camp you shall do just as I do: When I blow the trumpet, I and all who are with me, then you also blow the trumpets on every side of the whole camp, and say, 'The sword of the Lord and of Gideon!' "

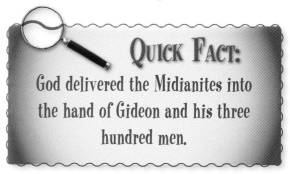

QUICK FACT: God delivered the Midianites into the hand of Gideon and his three hundred men.

Quietly the three groups of men advanced and surrounded the vast camp of Midian. At a signal from their commander, the three hundred men blew their trumpets and broke their pitchers. The torches gleamed brightly in the darkness. Then they shouted, "The sword of the Lord and of Gideon!"

The sleeping army woke up in terror. They saw gleaming torches everywhere, and the noise of the trumpets was deafening. Believing they were far outnumbered, the soldiers of Midian jumped up and ran. In the darkness and confusion they bumped into each other and began to fight and kill their own comrades. As the Midianite army fled, Gideon sent messengers to the surrounding territory to call for volunteers to chase the Midianites and destroy their forces. A great victory came to Israel, not by the strength of the sword but by the power of God.

SAMSON WANTS HIS OWN WAY

Judges 13–15:8

The tribe of Dan received as its inheritance the land stretching from Jerusalem west to the Mediterranean Sea. On the border of this region lived a powerful and blood-thirsty enemy, the Philistines. Four of the chief cities of these pagan people were Gaza, Gath, Ashdod, and Askelon.

Whenever Israel forgot about God and His protection was withdrawn, the Philistines would invade the farms and homes of the people of Dan. No road was safe because the enemy could attack anywhere. There were also times of peace, however, and in those times the Israelites traded with the Philistines. Some of the Israelite men disobeyed God's command to stay separate from the surrounding nations and married wives from among these idol-worshiping people.

One God-fearing man of the clan of Dan was named Manoah. He and his wife did not have any children. An angel appeared to his wife and told her that she would have a son. The boy should be brought up according to the strict rules of a Nazirite, the angel said. This meant that he should never drink any kind of alcohol nor eat unclean food. He must allow his hair to grow, and it should never be cut. Then the angel gave this promise: "He shall begin to deliver Israel out of the hand of the Philistines."

When the child was born, his mother named him Samson. He grew strong because the Spirit of God was with him. When Samson had grown to be a sturdy young man, he became restless. He left the family farm to visit the village of Timnah, across the border in the land of the Philistines. There he fell in love with a maiden, and when he came home, he said to his father and mother, "I have seen a woman in Timnah of the daughters of the Philistines; now therefore, get her for me as a wife."

His parents urged him to marry one of the girls from among his own people, a young woman who loved and worshiped the true God. They did not realize that God had His hand in Samson's choice, as a way to move against the Philistines. The son said to his father, "Get her for me, for she pleases me well."

Samson and his parents traveled to the Philistine village and came to the vineyards on the edge of the town. While they were visiting, Samson was walking alone when a young lion rushed at him and attacked him. The Spirit of God came over Samson, and he grabbed the savage beast and tore it apart with his bare hands. But he did not tell his parents what he had done. Soon his father and mother went back home.

> **GOD SAYS:**
> "So the woman bore a son and called his name Samson; and the child grew, and the Lord blessed him." –Judges 13:24

Samson stayed and visited the girl for a while, and then

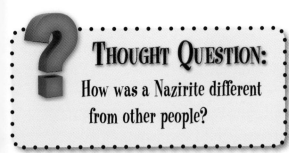

THOUGHT QUESTION:

How was a Nazirite different from other people?

he, too, set out for home. On the way he saw the carcass of the lion he had killed. When he looked at it closely, he found a swarm of bees in the carcass. He scraped out some of the honey and ate it as he walked along the road. Arriving home, he still had some of the honey and gave it to his parents. But he didn't tell them where it had come from.

Soon after this, Samson married the Philistine woman in her village, and among the guests at the wedding feast were thirty young men. To entertain these guests, Samson said, "Let me pose a riddle to you. If you can correctly solve and explain it to me within the seven days of the feast, then I will give you thirty linen garments and thirty changes of clothing. But if you cannot explain it to me, then you shall give me thirty linen garments and thirty changes of clothing."

"Pose your riddle," they said, "that we may hear it."

So he said to them,

"Out of the eater came something to eat,
And out of the strong came something sweet."

For three days the young men thought about the riddle, and they could not come up with the answer. On the fourth day of the feast, they threatened Samson's wife, saying, "Entice your husband, that he may explain the riddle to us, or else we will burn you and your father's house with fire. Have you invited us in order to take what is ours? Is that not so?"

So, Samson's wife cried on her husband's shoulder and begged him to tell her the answer. Her tears weakened him, and on the seventh day he told her the secret. She immediately went to the young men and gave them the answer to the riddle, which they still had not been able to solve.

The thirty men came to Samson and said,

"What is sweeter than honey?
And what is stronger than a lion?"

Knowing that his wife had let the secret out, Samson said,

"If you had not plowed with my heifer,
You would not have solved my riddle!"

The Spirit of God came over Samson, and he left the feast for Ashkelon, a Philistine city, where he killed thirty men and stripped them of their clothing. Then he returned to Timnah with the garments and gave them to the young Philistines to fulfill his bargain. He was so furious, however, that he went straight to his father's house, not stopping to see his wife.

Shortly after this, however, Samson took a present of a young goat and went to visit his wife. When he arrived, his father-in-law met him and would not let him into the house.

"I really thought that you thoroughly hated her," he said to Samson. "Therefore I gave her to your companion." The man meant that he had given Samson's wife to the best man from the wedding.

Now the strong young giant was really mad! He said, "This time I shall be blameless regarding the Philistines if I harm them."

He went out into the hills and caught three hundred foxes. With all three hundred of them, he put two foxes together tail to tail and then fastened a torch between the tails. Then he lit the torches and turned 150 pairs of foxes loose in the fields of the Philistines. They ran through the fields, setting on fire the wheat fields, the vineyards, and the olive groves. They destroyed everything of the Philistines.

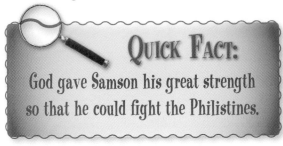

QUICK FACT:

God gave Samson his great strength so that he could fight the Philistines.

"Who has done this?" said the Philistines.

"Samson, the son-in-law of the Timnite," someone said. The word had spread that Samson's father-in-law had given his wife to another man.

In revenge the Philistines set fire to the house where Samson's wife lived and burned her and her father to death.

When he found out about the death of his wife, Samson came to the men of Timnah and said, "Since you would do a thing like this, I will surely take revenge on you, and after that I will cease." Then he attacked the men and killed many of them.

After this awful episode, instead of returning home, Samson went away and lived in the cave of Etam.

SAMSON IS BETRAYED

Judges 15:9–16:31

Samson! The name struck terror in the Philistines. They wanted to kill this mighty judge because he had done so much damage to their nation in such a short time. A band of Philistine warriors marched into the territory of Judah and set up camp. From there they conducted a raid on the town of Lehi.

"Why have you come up against us?" the Judeans asked.

"We have come up to arrest Samson," the Philistines answered, "to do to him as he has done to us."

Three thousand men of Judah went down to the cave at Etam and found Samson. They said to him, "Do you not know that the Philistines rule over us? What is this you have done to us?"

"As they did to me, so I have done to them," he replied.

"We have come down to arrest you, that we may deliver you into the hand of the Philistines."

Samson said to the men from Judah, "Swear to me that you will not kill me yourselves."

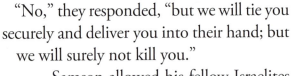

"No," they responded, "but we will tie you securely and deliver you into their hand; but we will surely not kill you."

Samson allowed his fellow Israelites to bind him with two pieces of new rope, and then they took him to the Philistines at Lehi. When the Philistines saw the men of Judah bringing the prisoner, they shouted at Samson and rushed out to meet them. The power of God came upon Samson, and he snapped the ropes that bound him as though they were stalks of dry flax. Seeing the jawbone of a donkey lying on the ground, he picked it up and attacked the Philistines, killing a thousand of them. Then Samson shouted triumphantly,

"With the jawbone of a donkey,
Heaps upon heaps,
With the jawbone of a donkey
I have slain a thousand men!"

Samson continued to be the judge of Israel. He had been judge for almost twenty years when he paid a visit to Gaza, the most important city of the Philistines. People who had seen him enter the city passed the word around: "Samson has come here!"

That evening, some men of Gaza went to the place where Samson was staying and waited for him. They said, "In the morning, when it is daylight, we will kill him." But at midnight Samson slipped past them and ran to the city gate, which was locked. He took hold of the large doors of the gate and the heavy gateposts and pulled them up, put them on his shoulders, and carried them to the top of a hill that faced Hebron. There he left them for the Philistines to find.

Although he was judge over Israel, Samson once again fell in love with a Philistine woman. Her name was Delilah, and she lived in the Valley of Sorek.

The Philistine chiefs came to her and said, "Entice him, and

find out where his great strength lies, and by what means we may overpower him, that we may bind him to afflict him; and every one of us will give you eleven hundred pieces of silver."

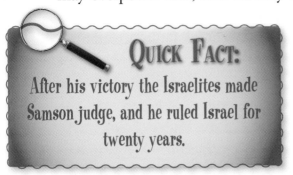

QUICK FACT:
After his victory the Israelites made Samson judge, and he ruled Israel for twenty years.

Delilah must have cared more about money than she cared about her boyfriend, because she went to Samson and begged, "Please tell me where your great strength lies, and with what you may be bound to afflict you."

Samson replied, "If they bind me with seven fresh bowstrings, not yet dried, then I shall become weak, and be like any other man."

Delilah told the Philistine chiefs what he had said, and they brought seven bowstrings to her, and she tied them around him. When the chiefs came into the house and tried to capture Samson, he snapped the bowstrings as if they were straw. So the source of his strength was not discovered.

Then Delilah said to Samson, "Look, you have mocked me and told me lies. Now, please tell me what you may be bound with."

So he said to her, "If they bind me securely with new ropes that have never been used, then I shall become weak, and be like any other man."

Delilah took new ropes and tied him up with them. Then she said loudly, "The Philistines are upon you, Samson!"

Some Philistines were hiding nearby, and they rushed into the room, but Samson snapped the ropes as if they were thread, and his enemies could not capture him.

The third time Delilah tried to obtain the secret from Samson, he told her that if his hair was woven into the web of a loom, he would lose all his strength. But that didn't work either, and a third time she failed to find out his secret.

Although she was thinking about the silver pieces she would receive from the Philistine chiefs, Delilah pretended to be hurt by Samson's jokes. "How can you say, 'I love you,' " she complained, "when your heart is not with me? You have mocked me these three times, and have not told me where your great strength lies."

The foolish man should have seen that Delilah was trying to betray him into the hands of his enemies. Over many days, she begged and whined and complained until Samson was exasperated, and to make her be quiet, Samson told Delilah the truth.

"No razor has ever come upon my head," he said, "for I have been a Nazirite to God from my mother's womb. If I am shaven, then my strength will leave me, and I shall become weak, and be like any other man."

Delilah was sure that he had finally revealed the secret to her, and she sent for the Philistine chiefs, saying, "Come up once more, for he has told me all his heart."

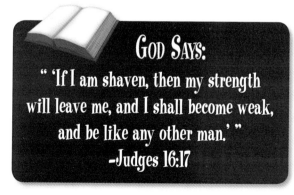

GOD SAYS:

" 'If I am shaven, then my strength will leave me, and I shall become weak, and be like any other man.' "

–Judges 16:17

Then the chiefs headed for Delilah's house with silver pieces in their hands. Meanwhile, she lulled Samson to sleep on her lap, and then she cut off all his locks of hair. She cried out, "The Philistines are upon you, Samson!"

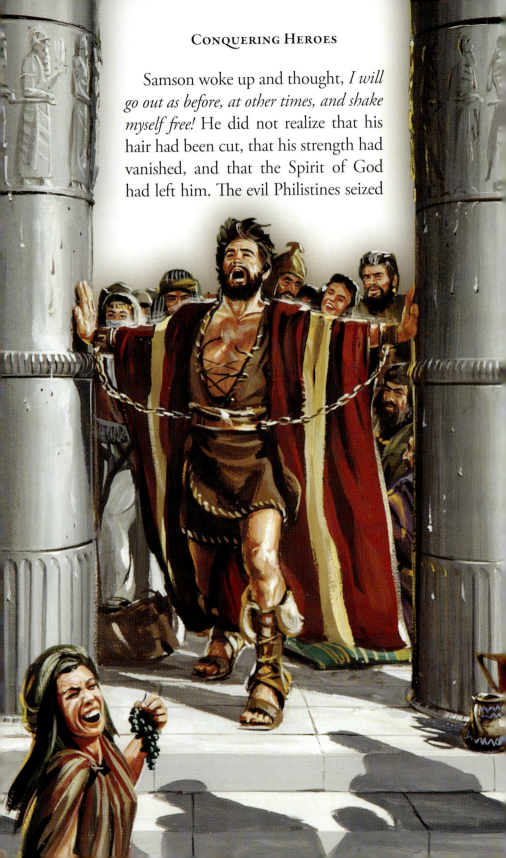

Samson woke up and thought, *I will go out as before, at other times, and shake myself free!* He did not realize that his hair had been cut, that his strength had vanished, and that the Spirit of God had left him. The evil Philistines seized

Samson, gouged out his eyes, and took him to Gaza. Poor blind giant! Now he was a helpless prisoner, bound with bronze shackles. He was forced to spend his days pushing the bar of a large grindstone to grind grain, as a slave would do.

But what happens after a haircut? Samson's hair began to grow back.

The famous English poet John Milton, who was also blind, imagined what Samson might have said in one of his magnificent poems:

> O glorious strength,
> Put to the labour of a beast, debased
> Lower than bondslave! Promise was that I
> Should Israel from Philistian yoke deliver;
> Ask for this great Deliverer now, and find him
> Eyeless in Gaza, at the mill with slaves,
> Himself in bonds under Philistian yoke . . .
>
> O loss of sight, of thee I most complain!
> Blind among enemies! O worse than chains . . .
>
> Life in captivity
> Among inhuman foes
> (John Milton, *Samson Agonistes,*
>   lines 36–42; 67, 68; 108, 109).

To celebrate the capture of mighty Samson, the Philistines held a lavish feast, at which they made offerings to their idol, Dagon. During their partying they said, "Our god has delivered into our hands Samson our enemy!"

The revelers shouted for blind Samson to be brought

into the feast for all to see. They said, "Call for Samson, that he may perform for us." Soon a boy appeared, leading the blind, unsteady giant. When Samson's enemies saw him, they laughed and jeered. Samson told the boy who was leading him, "Let me feel the pillars which support the temple, so that I can lean on them."

The hall was full of the lords and chiefs of the Philistines, about three thousand men and women altogether. Samson bowed his head and prayed to the God of heaven, saying, "O Lord God, remember me, I pray! Strengthen me, I pray, just this once, O God, that I may with one blow take vengeance on the Philistines for my two eyes!"

This was the man's last prayer. He braced himself against the two great pillars that supported the roof of the hall.

"Let me die with the Philistines!" Samson said, and with all his might he pushed the pillars. As they fell, the roof tumbled down with a terrible crash on the lords and all the other people below. "So the dead that he killed at his death were more than he had killed in his life," the Bible says.

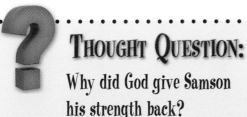

THOUGHT QUESTION:

Why did God give Samson his strength back?

Samson's relatives came for the body of the judge who had led Israel with great physical strength but weak willpower. They buried him in the family tomb near Zorah. Samson, who could not control his own habits and desires, might have written a much longer and more heroic chapter in the history of his people if he had always been true to God. But he forgot that the greatness of a man is measured not by physical ability but by self-control and obedience to the Spirit of God.

RUTH, GREAT-GRANDMOTHER OF A KING

Ruth 1–4

F amine struck the land of Canaan during the days of the judges. The parched ground baked in the hot sun; grain shriveled in the stalk. Fruit withered and fell from the trees, and the grass became brown in the pasture, worthless as food for the cattle and sheep. Similar famines had happened in the days of Abraham and Jacob. The early pioneers were forced to leave Canaan when these terrible famines struck.

Elimelech, a man of the tribe of Judah, lived in Bethlehem with his wife, Naomi. They had two sons, Mahlon and Chilion. When the crops failed and famine spread through the land, Elimelech decided to move southeast across the Jordan River to the land of Moab. In that foreign country the family lived for ten years. The two sons married young women of their neighborhood. One was named Orpah, the other Ruth.

Trouble came to the family during this time. Elimelech died, and soon afterward his two sons became sick and died. This left Naomi a widow in a foreign land with only her two daughters-in-law with her. She decided to return to her home in Bethlehem, because she had heard that the famine in Canaan was over.

As Naomi started on her journey home, Ruth and Orpah accompanied her. But when the woman thought about the future for the two young widows, she said, "Go, return each to her mother's house. The Lord deal kindly with you, as you have dealt with the dead and with me. The Lord grant that you may find rest, each in the house of her husband."

She kissed the two young women goodbye, and they began to weep. They said, "Surely we will return with you to your people."

Naomi replied, "Turn back, my daughters; why will you go with me?"

Orpah was persuaded by these words. She said Good-bye to her mother-in-law and returned to her own people. But Ruth had faith in the God of heaven, and she loved her mother-in-law. She said to Naomi,

> "Entreat me not to leave you,
> Or to turn back from following after you;
> For wherever you go, I will go;
> And wherever you lodge, I will lodge;
> Your people shall be my people,
> And your God, my God.
> Where you die, I will die,
> And there will I be buried."

The two women made the journey to Bethlehem, where they were greeted by Naomi's relatives and friends. When the people of Bethlehem saw their friend of former years,

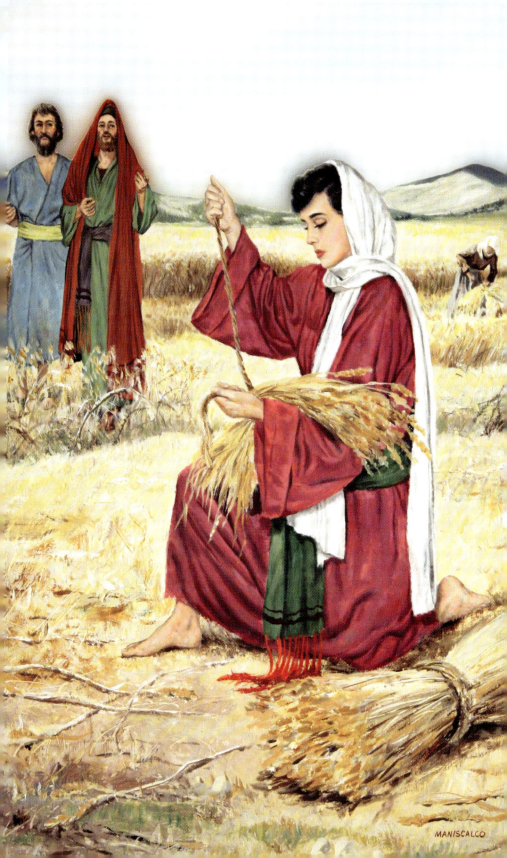

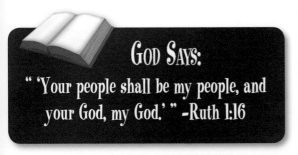

GOD SAYS:

" 'Your people shall be my people, and your God, my God.' " -Ruth 1:16

they were excited, and the women said to each other, "Is this Naomi?"

She said to them, "Do not call me Naomi; call me Mara, for the Almighty has dealt very bitterly with me. I went out full, and the Lord has brought me home again empty."

Naomi and Ruth found a home in Bethlehem at the beginning of the barley harvest. The laws of Israel required the owners of grain fields to allow poor people to glean the stalks of grain left behind by the reapers. They could also have the grain that grew in the corners of the fields.

Although the two women had a place to live, they needed food to eat. Ruth, knowing the law of the harvest, said to Naomi, "Please let me go to the field, and glean heads of grain after him in whose sight I may find favor."

So, Ruth went to glean in the field of Boaz, a wealthy relative of Naomi's husband. While she was picking up the grain that had fallen from the hands of the reapers, Boaz entered the field. He saw the beautiful woman and wondered who she was.

"Whose young woman is this?" Boaz asked the servant in charge of the harvesters.

"It is the young Moabite woman who came back with Naomi from the country of Moab," the servant answered.

The servant had noticed that Ruth was a diligent worker. He said to Boaz, "She came and has continued from morning until now, though she rested a little in the house."

Boaz walked over to Ruth and said, "You will listen, my daughter, will you not? Do not go to glean in another field, nor go from here, but stay close by my young women. Let your eyes be on the field which they reap, and go after them. Have I not commanded the young men not to touch you? And when you are thirsty, go to the vessels and drink from what the young men have drawn."

Ruth bowed down to the ground before Boaz and asked him, "Why have I found favor in your eyes, that you should take notice of me, since I am a foreigner?"

"It has been fully reported to me," Boaz replied, "all that you have done for your mother-in-law since the death of your husband, and how you have left your father and your mother and the land of your birth, and have come to a people whom you did not know before."

Boaz could not forget Ruth's sweet smile. At mealtime the man said to her, "Come here, and eat of the bread, and dip your piece of bread in the vinegar." Ruth seated herself beside the gleaners, and Boaz gave her some of the roasted grain to eat. It was a custom for the reapers to tie some of the stalks of grain in

QUICK FACT:
Israelite law demanded that the corners of the fields not be harvested and any grain that was dropped was to be left for the poor people.

bunches and roast them over the fire. When the grain was a rich brown, they would rub the ears in their hands and eat the roasted kernels.

After dinner, when Ruth had returned to her work, Boaz gave orders to his servants: "Let her glean even among the sheaves, and do not reproach her. Also let some grain from the bundles fall purposely for her; leave it that she may glean, and do not rebuke her."

At sunset Ruth hurried home with the grain she had gathered. "Where have you gleaned today?" her mother-in-law asked. "And where did you work? Blessed be the one who took notice of you."

"The man's name with whom I worked today is Boaz," she said.

"The man is a relation of ours," Naomi said to her, "one of our close relatives."

"He also said to me," Ruth continued, " 'You shall stay close by my young men until they have finished all my harvest.' "

"It is good, my daughter," Naomi said to her daughter-in-law, "that you go out with his young women, and that people do not meet you in any other field." The mother-in-law hoped that Boaz would continue to look with favor upon the beautiful girl.

Although Boaz was a relative of Elimelech, another man in Bethlehem was a closer relative to Naomi's husband. According to the law of Israel, if a man died without leaving children, the nearest relative had the right to purchase the family property, and he could also marry the widow. If the nearest relative did not wish to buy the land, the next nearest relative could do so. One day Boaz

went to the city gate, where the town's business was conducted, and sat down. Soon the man who was the nearest relative of Naomi's husband came by. Boaz called to him and told him about the land that should be redeemed. "There is no one but you to redeem

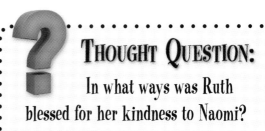

THOUGHT QUESTION:
In what ways was Ruth blessed for her kindness to Naomi?

it," Boaz said, "and I am next after you."

"I will redeem it," the relative said.

Then Boaz said, "On the day you buy the field from the hand of Naomi, you must also buy it from Ruth the Moabitess, the wife of the dead, to perpetuate the name of the dead through his inheritance." This meant that whoever redeemed the land would also marry Ruth.

"I cannot redeem it for myself, lest I ruin my own inheritance," the man replied. "You redeem my right of redemption for yourself, for I cannot redeem it. . . . Buy it for yourself."

An ancient custom in that land required that one man pull off his sandal and give it to the other to complete a business transaction. This was the way to seal an agreement. When the close relative said to Boaz, "Buy it for yourself," he took off his sandal and handed it to Boaz.

Then Boaz said to the city elders and the people standing by the gate, "You are witnesses this day that I have bought all that was Elimelech's, and all that was Chilion's and Mahlon's, from the hand of Naomi. Moreover, Ruth the Moabitess, the widow of Mahlon, I have acquired as my wife, to perpetuate the name of the dead through his inheritance."

The chief men and the other people witnessed the transaction and said to Boaz, "We are witnesses. The Lord make the woman who is coming to your house like Rachel and Leah, the two who built the house of Israel; and may you prosper in Ephrathah and be famous in Bethlehem."

Naomi, the aging mother-in-law, felt great happiness to see Ruth well married. Some time later the women of the neighborhood brought Naomi wonderful news. Ruth and Boaz had a baby son. The women said to Naomi, who was now a grandmother, "Blessed be the Lord, who has not left you this day without a close relative; and may his name be famous in Israel! And may he be to you a restorer of life and a nourisher of your old age."

Naomi went to Ruth's home and took the baby in her arms, rocking him tenderly. She became the baby's nurse, and she watched over him so lovingly that the neighborhood women teased her, saying, "There is a son born to Naomi."

The child's name was Obed. He became the grandfather of David, the mighty king of Israel.

THE BOY
PROPHET

1 Samuel 1–3

When the nation of Israel settled in Canaan, the tent of meeting was set up permanently at the city of Shiloh. Each year many of the faithful went there to worship God and to offer sacrifices and thank offerings.

Elkanah, a man from the town of Ramah, traveled to Shiloh to worship. He had two wives, Hannah and Penninah, who accompanied him each year to the tent of meeting. Penninah had children, but Hannah was childless. Hannah was their husband's favorite, and Penninah felt jealous. When Elkanah wasn't around, she often said mean things to Hannah about having no sons or daughters.

One year when the family visited Shiloh, Hannah cried and was depressed. She had not eaten anything all day. In the evening, Elkanah told her how much he loved her, saying, "Am I not better to you than ten sons?" But she still longed for a son. The next morning she went to the temple to pray. She made a vow to God that if she had a son, she would give him to the Lord for all the days of his life.

Eli, the high priest at the tent of meeting, saw Hannah standing near the entrance with her eyes closed. Her lips were moving, but no sound came out of her mouth. At first Eli thought she was drunk, but Hannah said to him, "No, my lord, I am a woman of sorrowful spirit. . . . Out of the abundance of my complaint and grief I have spoken until now."

Eli comforted her, saying, "Go in peace, and the God of Israel grant your petition which you have asked of Him." She returned to Elkanah's tent and ate with him, and her face no longer looked sad.

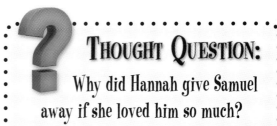

THOUGHT QUESTION: Why did Hannah give Samuel away if she loved him so much?

Sometime after the family returned to their home in Ramah, Hannah became pregnant and had a baby son. She named him Samuel, which means "Asked of God."

The years slipped by. When Samuel was old enough to leave home, Hannah kept her vow to God. She took the boy to the house of the Lord at Shiloh and presented him to Eli.

"O my lord!" she said to the high priest. "I am the woman who stood by you here, praying to the Lord. For this child I prayed, and the Lord has granted me my petition which I asked of Him. Therefore I also have lent him to the Lord; as long as he lives he shall be lent to the Lord." Elkanah's family worshiped God at the tent of meeting as they usually did, and Hannah prayed a beautiful prayer of thanks.

Little Samuel must have been homesick when his

mother left him. Eli was an old man, and with all of the work to do in God's house, there was little playtime for a boy who lived with the high priest. But Samuel did his work faithfully. He opened the doors of the house of God in the morning and closed them in the evening. He

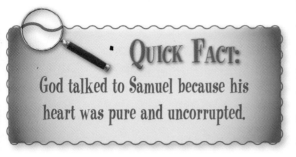

QUICK FACT:
God talked to Samuel because his heart was pure and uncorrupted.

kept the lamps trimmed, and he probably cleaned the floors and dusted the furniture in the high priest's living quarters.

Samuel wore a linen robe like the one the priests wore in their services. Each year when Hannah came to worship at the tent of meeting, she brought her son a new coat she had made with her own hands. Three more sons and two daughters were born to Hannah, so she was not lonely in her home anymore.

Samuel slept in the tent of meeting near where the lamps burned in front of the golden ark. One night he was aroused from a sound sleep by a voice calling his name.

"Here I am!" he replied.

He ran to Eli and said, "Here I am, for you called me."

"I did not call," Eli declared; "lie down again."

Samuel went back and lay down on his sleeping mat. Again a voice called out to him, "Samuel!"

Once more the boy arose and went to Eli's bed. "Here I am, for you called me," Samuel responded.

"I did not call, my son," replied the priest. "Lie down again."

When the voice called a third time, the boy got up quickly and went to Eli and said again, "Here I am, for you did call me."

Then Eli realized that it was the Lord calling the young boy. He said to Samuel, "Go, lie down; and it shall be, if He calls you, that you must say, 'Speak, Lord, for Your servant hears.' "

Until this time, Samuel did not know God and had never received a message from Him. The boy walked back to his bed and lay down. The Lord called again, "Samuel! Samuel!"

Samuel said, "Speak, for Your servant hears."

Then the Lord spoke these words to Samuel: "Behold, I will do something in Israel at which both ears of everyone who hears it will tingle. In that day I will perform against Eli all that I have spoken concerning his house, from beginning to end. For I have told him that I will judge his house forever for the iniquity which he knows, because his sons made themselves vile, and he did not restrain them. And therefore I have sworn to the house of Eli that the iniquity of Eli's house shall not be atoned for by sacrifice or offering forever."

> **GOD SAYS:**
> "So Samuel grew, and the Lord was with him and let none of his words fall to the ground." –1 Samuel 3:19

In the morning when Samuel opened the double doors of the house of the Lord, Eli called the boy to him and said, "Samuel, my son!"

"Here I am," he answered.

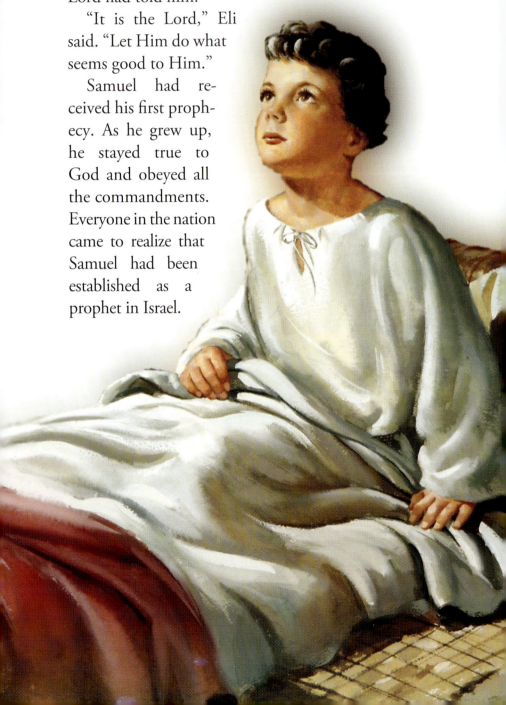

"What is the word that the Lord spoke to you?" he asked. "Please do not hide it from me."

Then Samuel told the high priest everything that the Lord had told him.

"It is the Lord," Eli said. "Let Him do what seems good to Him."

Samuel had received his first prophecy. As he grew up, he stayed true to God and obeyed all the commandments. Everyone in the nation came to realize that Samuel had been established as a prophet in Israel.

THE GOLDEN ARK IS CAPTURED

1 Samuel 4–7:2

N ew wars broke out between Israel and the Philistines. In a fierce struggle at Ebenezer, the army of Israel lost, and four thousand men died on the battlefield. When news of the defeat reached the people, the older men said, "Why has the Lord defeated us today before the Philistines? Let us bring the ark of the covenant of the Lord from Shiloh to us, that when it comes among us it may save us from the hand of our enemies."

The people sent some men to Shiloh, and with the help of Eli's two wicked sons, they took the golden ark from the tent of meeting. When the golden chest with the two beautiful angels on the cover was brought into the camp of Israel, all of the soldiers and the people gave a

QUICK FACT:
When the Israelites decided to take the ark into battle, they were using their own wisdom instead of depending on God's.

loud shout, which boomed and echoed across the valley to the camp of the Philistines. When the enemy soldiers heard the noise, they said, "What does the sound of this great shout in the camp of the Hebrews mean?"

Upon investigation they learned that the ark of the Lord had arrived at the camp. The Philistines were afraid, and they said to each other, "God has come into the camp!"

"Woe to us!" they said, "for such a thing has never happened before. Woe to us! Who will deliver us from the hand of these mighty gods? These are the gods who struck the Egyptians with all the plagues in the wilderness. Be strong and conduct yourselves like men, you Philistines, that you do not become servants of the Hebrews, as they have been to you. Conduct yourselves like men, and fight!"

This challenge to fight put courage into the Philistines, and they attacked Israel's army again. There was a terrible slaughter, and thirty thousand men of Israel fell that day, including the two sinful sons of Eli. In the overwhelming defeat, the golden ark was captured, and a roar of victory went up from the Philistine army.

A messenger ran to Shiloh to deliver the bad news. Eli the high priest, who was now ninety-eight years old and had gone blind, was sitting and waiting for news about the ark. His heart beat fast every time he thought of something bad happening to the sacred ark. Eli said to the runner, "What happened, my son?"

THOUGHT QUESTION:

Why did God allow the ark of the covenant to be captured?

Hurriedly the man told his story. "Israel has fled before the Philistines, and there has been a great slaughter among the people. Also your two sons, Hophni and Phinehas, are dead; and the ark of God has been captured."

This was more than the old priest could bear to hear. When the messenger told

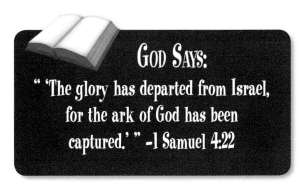

GOD SAYS:

" 'The glory has departed from Israel, for the ark of God has been captured,' " -1 Samuel 4:22

how the ark of the Lord had been taken, Eli fell backward off his seat, broke his neck, and died. Eli had been judge of Israel for forty years.

Meanwhile the Philistine armies marched back to their own country in a triumphant procession. They carried the golden ark to the city of Ashdod and placed it in the temple of their god, Dagon.

The next morning the people found that their idol had fallen facedown on the ground before the ark of the Lord. They lifted the idol and set it up in its place. The following morning the idol had fallen over again. This time its head and hands were broken off. Thousands of people in Ashdod began to get a terrible plague. So the leaders of the city said, "The ark of the God of Israel must not remain with us, for His hand is harsh toward us and Dagon our god."

They decided to send the ark to the city of Gath, but a widespread plague broke out in that city as soon as the sacred chest arrived. Then it was moved to Ekron, but when the ark arrived the people said, "They have brought the ark of the God of Israel to us, to kill us and our people!" Finally the chiefs of the Philistines held a council, and they gave an order: "Send away the ark of the God of Israel, and let it go back to its own place, so that it does not kill us and our people." The ark had been kept in the land of the Philistines for seven months.

Some Philistine men prepared a special peace offering and put it with the ark. They placed the golden chest on a cart drawn by two cows whose calves had been shut up in the barn. Without any encouragement, the cows left their calves behind and pulled the cart straight to the town of Beth Shemesh. Five Philistine chiefs followed the cart to see that it would arrive safely in the land of Israel.

The Israelites of Beth Shemesh were harvesting their grain in the field, and they looked up and saw the cart carrying the ark of the Lord toward them. The cows stopped in the field. Immediately the men of Beth Shemesh built an altar and

offered sacrifices to God on it. When the Philistine chiefs saw that the ark had arrived safely, they returned to their own country, thankful to be rid of the sacred object that had brought so much trouble to them.

Some priests came to the field and carried the golden ark to the home of Abinadab. Eleazar, his son, was given the job of caring for it.

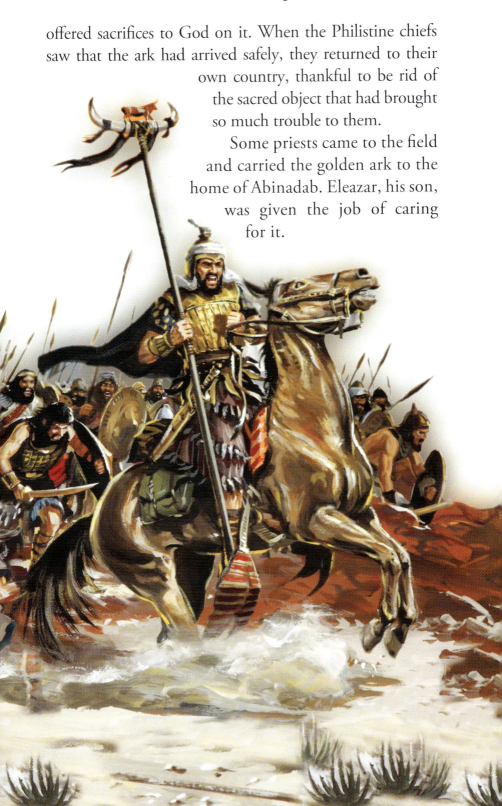

ISRAEL ASKS FOR A KING

1 Samuel 7:15–8:22

Samuel was the judge in Israel for many years. He made an annual tour from city to city, hearing complaints, making judgments, giving counsel, and teaching the people the way of God. When he grew old, Samuel made the serious mistake of establishing his two wicked sons as judges in the city of Beersheba. He should have learned a lesson from the evil conduct of the sons of Eli, but he loved his sons and was blind to their sins. They were greedy men, who took bribes from the people and made dishonest judgments.

When the people could not stand the evil of the sons any longer, Israelite leaders came to see Samuel at Ramah. They said to him, "Look, you are old, and your sons do not walk in your ways. Now make for us a king to judge us like all the nations."

THOUGHT QUESTION:

Why did the Israelites want a king?

This request troubled Samuel. He knew that it was not

in God's plan that the nation should have a king. He realized that when the people wished for a monarch, they were forgetting the Lord, their king in

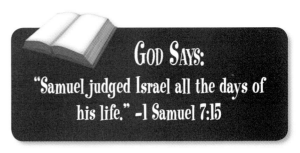

GOD SAYS:
"Samuel judged Israel all the days of his life." -1 Samuel 7:15

heaven. Samuel prayed about it, and God answered him by saying, "Heed the voice of the people in all that they say to you; for they have not rejected you, but they have rejected Me, that I should not reign over them. . . . Now therefore, heed their voice. However, you shall solemnly forewarn them, and show them the behavior of the king who will reign over them."

Samuel, the wise judge, told the people that when they had a king, their sons would be servants and their daughters would be cooks and bakers in the palace. He warned them that their lives would no longer be their own because a strong ruler would be a tyrant who controlled them. He would tax the nation heavily and make life miserable for the citizens. "And you will cry out in that day," Samuel concluded, "because of your king whom you have chosen for yourselves, and the Lord will not hear you in that day."

The people refused to listen to Samuel's counsel. They said, "No, but we will have a king over us, that we also may be like all the nations, and that our king may judge us and go out before us and fight our battles."

The Lord said to Samuel, "Heed their voice, and make them a king."

A new age was about to begin for the Israelites. They had been ruled by Moses, Joshua, and the judges who trusted in the Lord. From time to time God had sent His instruction directly to the leaders. Now the twelve tribes wanted to be like the nations around them. They had forgotten God and disobeyed His laws, which led them to try becoming great in their own strength. Knowing what would really happen later on, Samuel sent the people back to their homes to wait.